LOURDES COLLEGE LIBRARY

5560

D0877633

pl. 32

cv 3

WITHDRAWN

DUNS SCOTUS LIBRARY
LOURDES COLLEGE
SYLVANIA, OHIO

Evidence and Knowledge

SKILLS FOR CONTEMPORARY SOCIAL WORK

Tony Evans and Mark Hardy, *Evidence and Knowledge for Practice*

Andrew Hill, *Working in Statutory Contexts*

Evidence and Knowledge for Practice

TONY EVANS and MARK HARDY
with Ian Shaw

polity

Copyright © Tony Evans and Mark Hardy 2010

The right of Tony Evans and Mark Hardy to be identified as Author of this Work has been asserted in accordance with the UK Copyright, Designs and Patents Act 1988.

First published in 2010 by Polity Press

Polity Press
65 Bridge Street
Cambridge CB2 1UR, UK

Polity Press
350 Main Street
Malden, MA 02148, USA

All rights reserved. Except for the quotation of short passages for the purpose of criticism and review, no part of this publication may be reproduced, stored in a retrieval system, or transmitted, in any form or by any means, electronic, mechanical, photocopying, recording or otherwise, without the prior permission of the publisher.

ISBN-13: 978-0-7456-4339-7 (hardback)
ISBN-13: 978-0-7456-4340-3(paperback)

A catalogue record for this book is available from the British Library.

Typeset in 10.5 on 12 pt Sabon
by Toppan Best-set Premedia Limited
Printed and bound in Great Britain by the MPG Books Group

The publisher has used its best endeavours to ensure that the URLs for external websites referred to in this book are correct and active at the time of going to press. However, the publisher has no responsibility for the websites and can make no guarantee that a site will remain live or that the content is or will remain appropriate.

Every effort has been made to trace all copyright holders, but if any have been inadvertently overlooked the publisher will be pleased to include any necessary credits in any subsequent reprint or edition.

For further information on Polity, visit our website: www.politybooks.com

Contents

Introduction

This book is about how different sources of knowledge can be used to guide your work as a professional social worker. Social work is about helping people in society. To be helpful in any situation you need to work out what is going on and what you can do about it. As a professional social worker you will have the advantage of being able to draw on a range of established knowledge: ideas, theories, and sources of research. But how do you know which is the best advice, or which is the best way to help? How do you choose the appropriate course of action in a particular situation? These apparently straightforward questions give rise to a number of answers, because there are different ideas about the purpose of social work, about the way social workers can help, and about their aims in seeking to help people.

When you start in social work, you are often faced with a wide range of bodies of knowledge and expertise about practice. The idea that social work is fluid and diverse can be daunting. Sometimes it feels as if the only way to cope is to opt for one particular set of fixed rules of action, based on the 'correct' viewpoint. However, while this might be a convenient starting point, it quickly becomes apparent that practising social work is actually a messy business: it challenges rigid approaches and predetermined solutions. Social workers are people, who work with other people; and we all know that there is more to people than first meets the eye. Both people and practice are complex.

Commonplace complexity

In social work, complexity often lies in seeing what is always there, below the surface; recognizing the wider implications of apparently ordinary actions; acknowledging the important part played by feelings, thoughts and values in people's lives. There are always things going on that we don't know about. Take, for example, the following fictitious situation, which is an amalgam of some of our experiences in practice.

> Mrs Jones is 65 and suffers from chronic health problems, including arthritis and leg ulcers. She's had a community nurse for the past year, and they did seem to have developed a positive relationship. Recently, however, they have fallen out, and Mrs Jones has refused to let the district nurse visit, describing her as a busybody who sticks her nose into other people's business. (The disagreement developed after the nurse told Mrs Jones she must drink more water and look after herself.)
>
> Not long ago Mrs Jones tripped over a paving stone, and was admitted to Accident and Emergency. She didn't suffer any worse physical injuries than bruises and scratches, but she was shaken and her confidence was knocked. Mrs Jones also had an 'accident' in A&E, because she couldn't reach the toilet in time.
>
> After Mrs Jones left hospital, because she refused contact with the community nurse, her doctor made a referral to social workers, expressing concerns for her as a vulnerable adult, and asking for her to be assessed for residential care. The doctor is worried that she won't accept community services and has become uncooperative; that, in light of her fall, she is now neglecting her health care and is in danger of hurting herself; and that she is incontinent.
>
> Mrs Jones, on the other hand, insists that she is perfectly capable of looking after herself.

Mrs Jones's situation is a common scenario for social workers. They often have to work with people who are described as vulnerable or 'at risk', whom other services have sought to help but no longer feel able to do so. As a practitioner, you are required to work out what the important facts are, all the different perspectives of what has happened, and then what action to take. In Mrs Jones's case, there are several issues which need clarifying, and you need to decide how to approach them.

Take, for instance, her 'accident' in A&E. Did she wet herself because her arthritis prevented her from reaching the lavatory in time? Was there a queue? Is it fair to describe her as 'incontinent', which implies that there may be a physiological problem? Or was the problem that A&E's lavatories were few and far between? Similarly, did Mrs Jones fall in the first place because she is liable to fall (and doesn't look after her health by drinking enough water)? Or because of a broken paving stone, which was an accident waiting to happen? Even listing the 'facts' of this case is not a straightforward task: the selection and priority of facts depends on your view of which knowledge counts most. Two social workers might respond in two entirely different ways to this situation. For instance, should the focus be on Mrs Jones, or on the context of her case? If you see Mrs Jones's incontinence as the problem, then your solution may involve preventative work with her, to help her manage her illness. Alternatively, if you find that the fundamental problem is the lack of toilet facilities in A&E – and the subsequent queue to use them – your response might be to advocate with Mrs Jones, questioning the way she's been labelled as having a health problem, and challenging the lack of facilities in A&E.

However, the problem of complexity goes beyond identifying a framework through which to make sense of Mrs Jones's situation. It also involves recognizing that, whatever the choice of theory, this has a cost. Any solution means editing out aspects of the situation and in some way delineating the context. Mrs Jones may have been slow in getting to the toilet because of her arthritis. But there may also have been inadequate provision of toilets in A&E. Furthermore, Mrs Jones's behaviour may need to be understood in the context not just of the immediate circumstances, but also of her history – she may have felt unable to seek help from a nurse because she now viewed health professionals as interfering and intrusive.

Complexity, then, is not only about finding an explanation which best fits the circumstances; it is also about recognizing that explanations often prioritize certain aspects of what's going on at the cost of others. To get a full sense of a situation, it is necessary to bring different perspectives together.

The challenges thrown up by the everyday complexity of practice involve recognizing that people feel things, think about their situations in different ways, and exist in a network of social relations. As a social worker, you have to look at situations from a range of perspectives. You have to be able to work at the level of the presenting problem; but you also have to recognize that there may be a lot going on below the surface or in a broader context. You also have to negotiate people's rights to determine the services they want and your duties to intervene and override their autonomy and privacy. New problems, requiring new approaches, are thrown up all the time in social work, and you have to be ready to think on your feet. This is what makes social work both demanding and rewarding.

Professionalism, complexity and knowledge

If social workers are going to ask for trust and the right to use discretion – to demand, in other words, a professional status – they have to make this claim in a way that acknowledges and can accommodate the context of complexity as outlined above.

It's difficult to pin down what a 'professional' is. But one idea that's widely shared is that professionals are knowledgeable, and have the freedom to exercise their expertise (Noon and Blyton 2002). Their professional expertise lies in their ability to justify the course of action they propose to take, in relation to an established body of knowledge. The claim to knowledgeable expertise also relates to the idea that professionals should have discretion and the freedom to use their judgement in their practice. The claim that a social worker knows what to do is important, not only as the basis for sound practice, but also to back the demand to be left alone to get on with the job.

Complexity is an abiding characteristic of social work. Throughout its history, social work has struggled to pin down its definition. This struggle has frequently been expressed in disputes about the bodies of theory and knowledge on which social workers should draw (e.g. Timms 1983; Harris 2008).

An example of this process is the Barclay Report on 'Social workers: their role and tasks' (National Institute of Social Work 1982). The Barclay Committee was set up to answer a question which had been left by the Seebohm Report. The Seebohm Committee had recommended the establishment of social services departments (in England and Wales) as a home for social work, but had not explained what social work involved in any detail. Barclay sought to answer this question. The report produced turned out to be in three sections – a main report and two minority dissenting reports. Each of the dissenting reports put forward a different view of social work. One emphasized community social work; the other, social work as individual case-work.

The majority report rejected these two polar views, and sought to present a more inclusive view, which saw social work as engaging with both private struggles and public issues:

social workers are needed to carry out two different but interlocking activities. The first is to plan, establish, maintain and evaluate the provision of social care...planning with their clients – be they groups, individuals or families – provision of care to suit their particular needs.

The second activity which social workers are needed to provide is that of face-to-face communication between clients and social workers, in which social workers are helping clients to tolerate, or to change, some aspect of themselves or of the world in which they are living...[social work] demands a rejection of the idea that one part of a person in need can be isolated from other parts, that the person can be separated from other people and treated in a vacuum, or that the material and structural aspects of a problem can be separated from the emotional...the nature of social work knowledge, as one of those who sent us statements made clear, 'is concerned not just with a depth of understanding of a specialised and narrow area but with a comprehension of some of the ways in which different areas interact with and affect each other...The objective in view is the acquisition of a synthesis of knowledge which approaches more closely the totality of the client in his situation than any narrower approach can do'. (ibid.: 33–5)

Following on from Barclay, there have been numerous further attempts to specify what social work is and what social workers should know. However, the idea that social work is more than just one approach – which is central to the Barclay vision – has persisted, and continues to be reflected in official accounts of social work. In a recent review of social work 'Social work at its best: A statement of social work roles and tasks for the 21st century' by the GSCC (2008), Barclay's conception survives of social work as a complex process operating at various social levels.

Social work is committed to enabling every child and adult to fulfil their potential, achieve and maintain independence and self-direction, make choices, take control of their own lives and support arrangements, and exercise their civil and human rights. It looks at people's lives and circumstances in the round...(ibid.: para. 6)

[it]...makes a particular contribution in situations where there are high levels of complexity, uncertainty, stress, conflicts of interest, and risk, particularly to children and vulnerable adults. It applies specialist analytical skills and knowledge to assessing these situations, and making complex judgements on action to take. In some situations, decisions are necessary on whether or not to use statutory powers to intervene. (ibid.: para. 6)

Following from this discussion, our approach in this book will not be to argue that there is one correct body of professional knowledge. Rather, it will be to say that there are different ideas of professional knowledge; that these forms of knowledge can all contribute to good professional practice; and that good professional practice is based on a clear understanding and thoughtful use of different bodies of knowledge and their strengths and weaknesses.

Two points arise from this discussion that are relevant here. The first is that we have to address a possible criticism. This criticism is that social work has failed to focus; and that, to be effective, it has to draw on a sound body of scientific knowledge. According to this approach, the problem of complexity only exists because of fuzzy thinking.

Given that we can answer this first criticism, a second arises: in a context of complexity, how should we handle diverse knowledge?

The science of social work?

The idea of professional status is closely tied up with an occupational group's claim to have useful knowledge, and to use that knowledge in the interests of the people it serves. This links to the first issue we need to consider; that is the idea that, if only social work were clearer about what it knows, it would be clearer about what it should do. Some critics would say that eclecticism, a pick-and-mix approach to knowledge, doesn't reflect complexity; it reflects confusion or a nihilistic rejection of reality. According to this approach, what social work needs to do is to acquire a proper scientific knowledge base, distinguishing sound from unsound knowledge, on the basis of scientific criteria. 'It is almost superfluous to ask why social work should take on the character of science. It is hardly a question of "may or may not". Rather, should we say, it is a matter of the categorical *must*' (Thyer and Wodarski 2007: 23).

Thyer and Wodarski believe that through the employment of rational techniques it is possible to identify 'material causes' for social problems 'that do not rely on supernatural or metaphysical mechanism' (ibid.: 3). A problem here is the idea of 'material causes'. What does it mean? We can identify events that come together, but observing cannot find a cause (never mind a 'material cause'); all we can do is see the conjunction of events. We can't actually *see* a cause: it's an idea, an attempt to explain a relationship between factors we have identified (Hume 1970).

A view of science that has been influenced by this criticism of cause as a material fact is the work of the philosopher of science Karl Popper (Popper 2002; Magee 1997). Many modern exponents of evidence-based practice link their approach to Popper's philosophy (e.g. Sheldon 2001).

Popper describes the scientific method as a process of imaginative thought which is tested, ultimately to the point of destruction. Science involves making informed guesses about how the world works, and then seeking out information – not to prove these guesses right (there's always a chance that new information will emerge and undermine positive claims to possess 'the truth'), but to refute the predictions that emerge from theories: to actively seek to disprove ideas. If disproved, they are discarded; if not, they still have provisional value until their refutation.

This image of science is compelling, but it raises significant questions. Practically, what evidence does it take to refute a theory? Is one contradictory event sufficient? Or does there have to be a repeated pattern? If contradictory information arises, should the theory be totally discarded, or should it be retained and amended in some way to take account of the new information?

Scientific knowledge is driven by theory. Evidence does not prove a theory; rather, it tests it. The absence of contradictory evidence makes it possible to hold an idea about the world. But this does not necessarily prove other theories wrong.

These theoretical points lead us into a fundamental question about scientific knowledge and its claims, namely: *is this how science actually operates in practice?*

Thomas Kuhn (1970), a leading historian of science, has argued that the history and development of science is a story of the disjointed progression of 'paradigms', and contrasts this with the usual view that science has of itself as the continual progress from ignorance to knowledge.

Established science – what Kuhn calls 'normal science' – is much more conservative and uncritical when compared with Popper's ideal picture of science. Those engaged in the scientific enterprise are committed to a view of the world – paradigms – which they seek to prove and justify by adopting methods of enquiry that most comfortably fit with their assumptions. Paradigms, Kuhn explains, are shared views of what scientific enquiry involves, what science should study, how it should be studied and what the goals of study should be. In contemporary social work a scientific approach emphasizes measurement and specification. It studies interventions, which should be clear and specific, and it is critical of vague global claims.

By seeing the world in this way, and requiring those who describe themselves as social workers to see it in the same way, evidence-based practice attempts to establish itself as 'normal science', the paradigm of contemporary professional social work. However, the downside of 'normal science' is that it is rigid, inward-looking and dismissive of alternative approaches. To make progress, it has to ignore other problems: it is only interested in what it knows. Anything outside what it sees as 'normal' scientific knowledge or practice is dismissed as unscientific.

For Kuhn, normal science can create knowledge; but it does this at the cost of confusing a useful, but limited, way of looking at the world to solve particular problems, with the world itself. Belief in the paradigm involves uncritical acceptance of basic assumptions, and ignoring those who don't share these assumptions. Normal science is: 'addressed only to professional colleagues, the men whose knowledge of a shared paradigm can be assumed and who prove to be the only ones able to read the papers addressed to them' (ibid.: 20).

According to Kuhn, science can adapt and develop, but it does so in seismic shifts. It is committed to certain theories; and it only changes when it loses confidence in its preferred theories – when its adherents can no longer explain away anomalies or persuade themselves that the great breakthrough is just over the horizon. However, Kuhn does identify a point in the scientific process between the supremacy of one paradigm and another, when several viewpoints contend and operate alongside one another, offering a choice and engaging with the fragmented and complex nature of the world. Kuhn sees this process as an important and valuable aspect of science. It's a process which creates innovation. It's an equally valid approach to knowledge, and one which he sees as playing a significant role not only in science but also in other areas of life. Here, knowledge is fluid and involves explaining and exploring assumptions, and looking at different ways of seeing and understanding the world. In science, Kuhn points out that this creative approach involves engaging with different observations and forms of knowledge, and: 'under these circumstances, the dialogue of the resulting books was often directed as much to members of other schools as it was to nature. That pattern is not unfamiliar in a number of creative fields today, nor is it incompatible with significant discovery and invention' (ibid.: 13).

This approach to knowledge seems to be particularly appropriate when we talk about the social world. Its emphasis on dialogue offers the opportunity for a recognition of its subject matter as human agents, where the subjects of study in the social world are able to challenge and question assumptions made about them by investigators.

Discourses of professional knowledge

This argument may seem distant from the practical knowledge that social workers need in their day-to-day work. But it offers an approach to understanding professional knowledge which seeks to engage with a complex world, where shoehorning reality into one perspective can shut off other options. Kuhn's analysis of the way science operates provides a useful way of negotiating the extremes of either equating knowledge with dominant 'normal science', or seeing all knowledge as equally valid. Rather, his notion of perspectives in conflict suggests that we understand knowledge as valid within contexts; that knowledge (and the means of acquiring it) may work well in one context but less usefully in another.

Increasingly, the analysis of professionalism has focused on understanding professions as occupations located within networks of beliefs, practices and commitments, which discipline and direct the activity of the professional group and promote certain views of knowledge (Fournier 1999; Evetts 2006). Rather like Kuhnian paradigms, these systems of professional knowledge seek to focus professional work in certain areas, emphasizing particular commitments, sources of knowledge and ways of practising professionally.

This analysis is useful in understanding debates within a profession, such as social work about its purpose and nature. Different ideas of knowledge relate to different priorities for practice. It's by examining arguments about different forms of knowledge in their context – particularly ideas of what gives practice status and legitimacy – that we can understand the relationship between 'valid knowledge', professional accountability and professional conduct. Recognizing this helps us to understand that many disputes about knowledge are actually disputes about the nature and role of social work, and arguments about the role of social work are also about which form of knowledge it is legitimate for professionals to employ.

An example of such a dispute in the modern welfare state focuses on ideas of whether social workers are policy-implementers or clinicians: is social work a discipline informed by the organizations within which it is located (and therefore centrally concerned with policy knowledge)? Or is it a clinical discipline, informed primarily by psychological theories?

In 1959, social scientist Barbara Wootton (1959) criticized the shift she saw in social work from practical social administration to clinical practice emphasizing psychological theory. In the appendix to Wootton's book *Social Science and Social Pathology*, her research assistant Rosalind Chambers notes:

> In most professions a decisive factor in the status of individuals or groups is that there are established and definite criteria of competence, required not only by the profession, but also by the community. In social work such definitions are less commonly accepted, and the position has become more obscure since the emphasis in case work shifted from the relief of various forms of need to the vague regions of maladjustment and personal relationships. Formerly, as the welfare state with its volume of social legislation impinged increasingly upon the life of the citizen, it was necessary for the social worker to possess full and accurate knowledge if satisfactory advice were to be given to the client, and her capacity and qualifications could be assessed by the result of her activity. But now the emphasis is predominantly on social relationships, diagnosis and cure are more vague and questionable, although the apparatus of 'know how' and the professional vocabulary are more elaborate than ever before. (Chambers 1959: 355)

Half a century on, this dispute about professional knowledge and practice continues. Wilson et al. (2008) are critical of contemporary social work, which they characterize as dominated by a concern for social policy knowledge and tasks. They argue that this approach lacks personal engagement with service users; that it is too rational, distant and bureaucratic. Instead, they put forward a different way of practising social work, which draws on a different body of knowledge. For them social work should be a 'relationship-based' profession, which:

> is closely related to and builds on psychosocial approaches to practice and psycho dynamically informed casework tradition. The central characteristic of relationship-based practice is the emphasis it places on the professional relationship as the medium through which the practitioner can engage with and intervene in the complexity of an individual's internal and external worlds. (Wilson et al. 2008: 7)

These quotations illustrate the interconnection of arguments about knowledge and about professional roles. This is not just a debate within social work; it is also the presentation of social work to the public as a valid profession. This brings us to the idea of professional status as a bargain between society and an occupational group. The occupational group gains status, freedom and rewards; society gains access to its expertise. However, society is not a unified whole. Powerful groups are able to promote their own interests by supporting certain professional ideas.

In the 1980s, radical political changes affected social work directly, questioning its value. Brewer and Lait (1980) published a study that fundamentally questioned the effectiveness and purpose of social work. Their critique resonated with the Conservative government's concerns about social work and the 'drooling and drivelling' nature of the welfare state (Thatcher, quoted in Aldridge 1996: 182). In this political context the advocates of behavioural social work put their approach forward, not only as a critique of and alternative to approaches to practice within social work but also as a response to the question advanced by Brewer and Lait *Can Social Work Survive?* They argued that casting social work in terms of learning theory would save it as a profession. By presenting it as an occupation that could specify and measure its work, advocates of behavioural social work, sought to defend social work's professionalism and avoid its collapse into a narrow, administrative role (Hudson and Macdonald 1986). This theme of framing social work in terms of the political concerns of particular governments has continued – for instance, in arguments for empirical-based practice and evidence-based practice, which specifically link the value of this approach to statements by government ministers: 'The commitment to evidence-based medicine pervades medical practice. This kind of commitment should be extended to the social services world' (Dorrell 1996, quoted Macdonald 2003: 1).

Claims about legitimate knowledge for practice are political, both in the sense of relating to disputes within professions about the nature of professional activity; and in the relationship between the concerns of the profession and wider social and political interests. The important point here is to set these claims in the context of our earlier discussion about the complexity of practice; and to be sceptical of any assertion that there is only one right way to practise, one right form of knowledge for practice. Professional bodies of knowledge should aim to assist practitioners to make sense of the world around them, and offer practical support. Knowledge is a means to an end. It's a way of being able to help. Where you're dealing with complexity, knowledge is likely to be complex and fragmented. Traditionally, social work knowledge has tended to emphasize particular focuses and related forms of knowledge with quality of practice defined in terms of practice conforming to theoretical precepts.

In fact, a common criticism of practice has been that it seems to be a pick-and-mix eclecticism, lacking theoretical rigour. This argument would be compelling if it were accompanied by a clear demonstration that the world with which social work engages conforms to the theoretically exacting picture of practice that its advocates profess. However, it's unlikely that any one role or form of knowledge is sufficient by itself to capture the nature of the social world or to provide sound knowledge for social work practice.

Recognizing that different perspectives are the result of our limited ability to capture the world, or of the blinkers we wear to deal with it, is a major step in seeing different ideas of knowledge as resources we can use in practice. The key skill we think you need as a social worker is to understand the concerns, assumptions and insights of different viewpoints, so that you can make informed judgements in your practice. You need to be able to think creatively.

As a social worker you don't just need to know about the evidence base for specific interventions, or how to engage in effective therapeutic relationships or identify and address structural oppression. A focus on one particular aspect of a problem or one body of knowledge as the 'right' way often means moving away from the complexity of practice to force it into a narrow and restricted way of working. For instance, the idea that social workers are just working with policy and putting it into effect fails to take account of the fact that the impact of poverty on a person may not just be material; over time, it can sap a sense of self and personal dignity, calling for an understanding of its emotional, as well as its practical impact.

This discussion has touched on an important idea that we need to note. These perspectives, while they may produce different ideas about our understanding of 'reality', offer a range of insights that reflect various concerns and views about what it is to be human and engaged in social projects with fellow human beings. In this sense ethical questions are closely interwoven into questions of our knowledge of the social world (Norman 1998). Utilitarianism, for instance, is the idea that moral judgements involve balancing diverse and conflicting needs based on the calculation of the greatest good; and this tends to tie in with the idea that we can quantify individuals' notions of 'good' and add up these views to reach a correct course of action. In contrast to this, rights-based approaches tend to focus on the idea of fundamental human attributes, which are universal and give rise to inalienable rights. In general each of these perspectives tends to foreground different forms of knowledge – utilitarianism, a knowledge which can quantify and calculate outcomes; and the rights-based approach, a knowledge that can specify and detail fundamental human qualities.

We want to avoid portraying certain approaches to knowledge as moral, and others as not. This would be too simplistic, not to say misleading. But this is an issue that needs careful consideration, because in social work, as in other fields, the claim to 'professionalism', which justifies the use of discretion and authority, relies on a combination of the idea of expertise, and a commitment to the use of this expertise for ethical ends. Accordingly, in this book we have not approached the idea of ethical knowledge as a separate issue, but have sought in our discussions of different knowledge to examine not only technical questions but also key ethical issues.

The struggle for professional practice is to maintain the sense that knowledge provides tools to engage with complexity – and not to force a complex world into a 'one size fits all' framework. Professionalism in social work, as Aldridge notes, must involve a critical approach to knowledge:

> Recent history is littered with episodes where new practice paradigms have been adopted wholesale and uncritically. Too often, social workers have been transformed into the unarmed consumers of intellectual marketing precisely because there is so little robust discussion of ideas. Good 'theory' is not mere mystification, a meal ticket to be dumped as soon as qualification is attained. It is a central occupational dynamic, as practitioners analyse what is of wider relevance from their daily experience, exchange and refine it. (Aldridge 1996: 190)

Conclusion

In short, this book's approach is to be sceptical of the assumption that there is one 'right' way to do social work. Social work practice is too complex simply to be captured and contained by one body of knowledge. Social workers deal with dynamic and diverse situations, where there are structured inequalities. In practising social work professionally, you will need to be able to draw on a range of ways of understanding people in their various social situations, as well as understanding your own impact on and relationship with them. And for us the best way to work in this challenging environment is to recognize that any way of 'knowing' has strengths and weaknesses, practical and ethical. They are different perspectives that highlight different aspects of a situation.

Limiting yourself to one perspective curtails your ability to help.

Chapter 1 provides an overview of different sources of knowledge – organizational, service-user, practitioner, research, and policy. It considers these in relation to a framework commissioned by SCIE, which aims to provide a set of criteria by which to evaluate forms of knowledge (Pawson et al. 2003). The following four chapters look at particular forms of knowledge, and how they relate to social work practice.

Chapter 2 looks at evidence-based practice as a key form of knowledge concerned with the evaluation of social work interventions. The third chapter looks at knowledge drawn from the expertise and experience of service-users and carers, and considers its role in advancing social work's commitment to empowerment and justice. Chapter 4 sets the debates in social work about knowledge in the broader context of the contemporary social science analysis of knowledge production. The fifth chapter looks at policy knowledge and how this relates to professional claims to expertise and discretion. Chapter 6 considers knowledge from practice, particularly the role of critical reflection in informing, guiding and developing social work practice.

These chapters explore current debates in key areas of knowledge. Chapter 7 looks at professional knowledge in the context of its organizational setting. Social work, like most professional activities, tends to occur within organizations, and the intersection of professional commitments and organizational requirements is a crucial dynamic. Chapter 8 argues that approaches to doing research inform practice, and explores this idea by considering how qualitative enquiry methods can be used to guide and develop direct work in the field.

The concluding chapter draws these themes together, arguing for an integrated approach to the use of knowledge and evidence in practice.

This book is a collaborative enterprise. It is intended as an introduction to an important, complex and sometimes contentious area of social work. We have sought to represent the range of debates in this book and in doing this our aim has been to learn to recognize that while there are areas where we may share views there are also areas where our views diverge. A book is a practical exercise and we have divided up primary responsibilities for drafting chapters. Mark

Hardy is the main author for the Chapters 1, 4, and 6 and the conclusion. Tony Evans is the main author of this introduction and Chapters 2, 3, and 5. We are also grateful to Ian Shaw who contributed Chapters 7 and 8 to the book. The book benefits from incorporating a range of voices which, we hope, provides added insight into a diverse and stimulating area of study and practice.

1

Knowledge: Philosophy, Theory and Practice

In this chapter we set the scene for what follows by exploring a number of related issues, including what knowledge is and different ways of thinking about what we know and how we might know. These are important issues for social workers given recent efforts to move their practice away from what might loosely be seen as a form of authority-based activity to one which is more explicitly knowledge based. Arguably, the purpose of evidence-based practice is to move from a situation in which practitioners make decisions and act on an individualized and subjective basis to a position in which these activities are informed and justified by reference to the wider knowledge base of the profession. A proper understanding of why this transformation might be occurring requires exploration of wider debates in the philosophy of social science, which, though hardly to the fore in day-to-day social work practice, nevertheless are crucial to understanding what social workers do, how and why. In what follows, then, we will concern ourselves with issues, concepts, debates and authors which may appear only distantly related to day-to-day practice, but which are nevertheless relevant to our purposes here. These include: the nature and status of knowledge; how knowledge is generated; paradigms, and distinctive paradigmatic positions; and, consequently, the work of key thinkers in the philosophy of science who have contributed to these debates.

We will then turn to how this debate has traditionally played out in social work, particularly as this relates to the purposes and utility of knowledge in practice, and the various types of knowledge which might underpin core social work tasks. There are competing positions in social work about the nature of knowledge, and how we know, which cluster around particular paradigmatic affiliations. A key issue is which – if any – of the various worldviews best reflects the nature of the social work enterprise and is thus best equipped to produce the kinds of knowledge that social work and social workers need to address both day-to-day practice issues and contemporary challenges. We relate such discussions to the position taken by SCIE (Pawson et al. 2003) in their influential typology of knowledge in social work, which in itself represents a distinctive take on these issues. As we shall see, concerns about the nature, status and forms of knowledge appropriate for practice are enduring and arguably irresolvable.

Knowledge

From a contemporary vantage point it may be difficult for many practitioners to envisage circumstances in which the decisions which they make in their day-to-day work might be anything but guided by up-to-date policy and protocols informed by the latest findings about how best to achieve the objectives of social work. Equally, they may well have been schooled in the view that contemporary practice represents the pinnacle of a process of evolutionary trial and error which cumulatively has led to the development of systems and procedures which operationalize knowledge regarding how best to proceed in particular situations. To an extent, they would be correct. Contemporary practice, and the legal and policy framework within which it occurs, tend to represent attempts to 'make real' state-of-the-art thinking. However, it also sometimes disguises or downplays the extent to which, despite this, these issues remain contested territory.

So what is knowledge? We all tend to have an intuitive understanding of what knowledge 'is'. It refers, surely, to what is 'known' about a particular subject. If only that were the case! In fact, universally accepted definitions are elusive. An entire branch of philosophy – epistemology, or the theory of knowledge – concerns itself with the nature and status of knowledge, which should alert us to the potential for controversy. The status of knowledge is, indeed, much argued over. This is apparent, for example, when we consider the suggestion that 'facts' represent knowledge which is not disputed – implying that much of what we refer to as knowledge is not factual, particularly in the social sciences, where key knowledge claims are endlessly debated. Suffice it to say that defining knowledge is less straightforward than might be assumed and that it is useful to bear in mind that it remains contested.

So if knowledge is not factual, then what status does it actually have? These are big issues, and major thinkers have sought to differentiate opinion, belief, truth, and facts for millennia. Our purposes here are more straightforward, and so we do not excessively problematize knowledge. A classical definition is provided by Shaw (2008: 186), who states: 'Something is knowledge if I believe it, my belief is justified, and it is true – knowledge on this reading is justified true belief.' Knowledge therefore stands in opposition to those beliefs or statements which are not justified or true. This conceptualization, however, represents an orienting device, rather than a definitive statement, not least because it offers little guidance as to how we might define either 'belief' or 'truth', nor which criteria we might use to assess whether these are justified. Michael Sheppard is correct to remind us that 'the nature of what constitutes knowledge is a matter of some disagreement, and this is a significant matter in considering when and how any form of knowledge may be used' (2004: 18). This is evident when we consider in more depth the nature of knowledge and how we might know.

Ontology and epistemology

In order to be able to arrive at a formulation of what knowledge is and how it may be understood, practitioners need an understanding of debates about the nature of knowledge, and how it is produced. The primary concern of ontology – again, a philosophical practice – is 'the theory of the nature of what is or the theory of the nature of reality' (D'Cruz and Jones 2003: 6). Debate centres on whether there is actually a 'real' world, or whether what we perceive to be real is instead an individual interpretation, itself informed by personal or cultural experiences and preferences. The key concern within epistemology, meanwhile, is with whether there is such a thing as knowledge which can be defined, identified and differentiated, with the debate centring on if and how it is ever possible to be certain that knowledge claims are true or accurate – or 'what is knowledge, and how we know' (Delanty and Strydom 2003: 1). 'Objectivists' argue that the world is real and that we can understand it, whereas 'subjectivists' regard 'reality', such as it is, as generated by individual subjects. Ontology and epistemology are commonly regarded as related, sometimes in a linear fashion, with ontological preferences informing epistemological issues, and also have implications for the methods via which knowledge might be generated. Distinctive positions which reflect these differing assumptions are commonly known as paradigms.

Exercise

Spend some time making sense of and answering the following questions:

Is there a 'real' world separate from your own thoughts and beliefs? How do you know? What evidence can you marshal in support of your views?

Paradigms

The concept of a paradigm refers to 'the entire constellation of beliefs, values, techniques and so on shared by members of a given community' (Kuhn 1970: 175). It equates to a basic set of beliefs that cohere as a worldview which underpins our decisions and actions in efforts to navigate our environment. Paradigms represent statements about what we know and how we know, and inform knowledge production in ways which are not always obvious. Put another way, our worldview – what we believe about the nature and status of reality, and how we can understand this – informs the way that we will go about identifying issues to investigate, as well as undertaking knowledge generation for this purpose. Arguably, certain paradigms are accorded more status within society, which has particular implications for social work, because its own 'worldview' is at odds with more dominant perspectives.

A note on terminology

We now turn to the nature and characteristics of these distinctive and sometimes competing paradigmatic positions, through discussion of positivism, interpretivism, critical theory and realism, respectively. The terminology which is utilized in philosophy can be off-putting for non-specialists. This is especially the case where terms are not used consistently. In what follows we will follow the organizing parameters laid out by Blaikie (2007), who specifies the fundamental ontological and epistemological disputes between alternative paradigmatic affiliations as being broadly between 'realist' and 'idealist' positions, but discusses these distinctions by reference to the more commonly used distinctions between positivism and interpretivism, critical theory and realism. Other authors may use different conventions, and readers should remain alert to the potential for confusion.

Science

Historically, concerns about knowledge have been closely related to the development of science. The physical and natural sciences seek to explain the world in terms of statistically based rules. Their significance to the development of society, especially since the Enlightenment in the seventeenth century, has ensured that the associated assumptions and methods hold a privileged position within our culture, as the benchmark for all forms of knowledge creation. We tend to think unproblematically in terms of the possibility of prediction, of problem-solving on the basis of what has gone before and of utilizing knowledge to further our ends. But what makes scientific knowledge distinctive? This is an important question, because the status of a knowledge claim as 'scientific' lends weight to the merits of that claim in ways which have meaningful effect.

Positivism

Science has traditionally been defined by reference to debates in the philosophy of science concerning the strengths and limitations of positivism as an exemplar of the scientific method against which the respective merits of competing alternatives can be assessed. Karl Popper, for example, assumed that the claims of science, though not without their limitations, nevertheless are distinctive, and sought to establish what was specific about this distinctiveness by reference to the ways in which theoretical propositions (hypotheses) were confirmed or refuted. Thomas Kuhn by contrast pointed to the contextual circumstances – history, culture, society – within which the criteria which are used to judge the status of knowledge are applied. Paul Feyerabend was yet more radical, suggesting that there is nothing of actual consequence which differentiates science from non-science, thus relegating scientific method to the position of just one of many potential ways of thinking about how knowledge might be developed.

The term logical positivism derives from a positive belief in the potential of scientific logic to contribute to the production of factual knowledge. It represented the dominant position within science, certainly until the mid twentieth century, and remains influential. Briefly, the ontological assumptions here are that there is an external reality, which is governed by natural laws. Epistemologically, the process of knowledge creation is seen as straightforward, in that it is both necessary and possible for researchers to be objective and for research findings – or 'knowledge claims' – to be made without subjective personal biases 'contaminating' knowledge. Irrespective of the merits of such claims, a key point of contention exists regarding the applicability of the assumptions and methods which have proved useful in studying the 'natural' world to the separate arena of 'the social'. Whereas science posits controlled laboratory conditions as an ideal environment for testing and proving knowledge claims, it is difficult and potentially unethical to replicate such conditions when studying humans, who have some degree of agency, or freedom to decide how to act, and are therefore capable of behaving according to individual preference, rather than merely obeying pre-set 'laws' of nature. Consequently, critics of positivism argue that human behaviour is not dictated by essentialist principles, according to law-like rules, but is the outcome of individual experience and perception.

Empiricism

Evidence derived from observation is one of the criteria which have traditionally been regarded as characteristic of scientific knowledge. Logical positivists argued that the best way of testing the substance of a knowledge claim was via experience, or empirically. This entails the development of explanatory hypotheses to account for some observed event and their revision where these are not supported. Empiricism represents an attempt to develop a model to verify those knowledge claims which are not immediately verifiable or discreditable just by logical argument. Verification was regarded as central to early versions of positivism.

Positivism, then, takes a particular position about how knowledge is produced and how the methods of production relate to the status of knowledge. Its key assumptions include the fundamental view that 'there is a basic unity to human experience and that we are therefore able to gain knowledge of reality and indeed construct a knowledge system about it' (Delanty and Strydom 2003: 13). The existence of knowledge enables us to make predictions and to manipulate the world to achieve ends. In theory, such knowledge is derived experientially and verified empirically by neutral, objective practitioners who bracket off subjective factors on the basis of a commitment to the importance of separating facts from values, or truth and belief

– the 'purpose' of knowledge, after all. Via the production and acqui-sition of knowledge, the aim is to improve society progressively. Central to scientific method are the verification of hypotheses and inductive reasoning.

Theory

Theories are developed and act as the basis of 'laws' or 'rules' per-taining to phenomena. It is important to be aware of the distinction between empirical and normative theories and how best to generate or test these. While factual statements, about how things *are*, are verifiable via recourse to empirical methods, normative statements, about how we think things *should* be, derived from ethics and values, cannot be verified or refuted by experience (empiricism). Logical positivists maintained that it is a concern with knowledge claims which are verifiable which is the province of science, while knowledge concerning normative issues – which are not verifiable – is beyond the scope of science. Ethical issues, then, concerning what is right or wrong, are not resolvable via the methods of science. They 'generate endless disputes that are ultimately unfruitful' (Bortolotti 2008: 9) as 'ethical statements…are only preferences that are ultimately subjec-tive and often clash with the preferences of others' (ibid.). This is not a view with which we are usually comfortable – we tend to think that our values are not just highly individualized preferences, but carefully developed positions which reflect the weighing up of com-peting options regarding what is right and proper that others ought to share. The positivist position – that ethics are indisputably meta-physical in nature – and that it is method which differentiates the two – is therefore, for some, discomfiting. Arguably, though, it is indisputable.

Reasoning

There are two 'standard' varieties of reasoning, the deductive and the inductive. Knowledge is produced in different ways according to whichever logic is privileged. The deductive approach entails 'theory testing' and the inductive approach entails 'theory building'. In the former case, hypotheses are derived from a pre-existing theoretical perspective, and tested. This is often via 'observation', which con-firms or refutes the hypothesis. The latter, by contrast, starts with data, from which emerging patterns are identified, which contribute to the development of theory. These approaches to knowledge generation tend to be affiliated with particular paradigmatic positions.

Less commented upon, but of particular relevance to social work, is a further style of reasoning known as 'inference to the best explanation', whereby a choice is made between competing explanatory hypotheses. Here, a particular theoretical perspective seems accurate given the circumstances, but is acknowledged as by no means certain. A 'best fit' between what is known and what is uncertain is aspired to, though ultimately the decision made will be based upon non-scientific, subjective preferences.

Necessarily, then, neither induction or inference to the best explanation can be regarded as logically valid in the way that knowledge derived from the deductive style of reasoning may. This is not to suggest, however, that they are not of value, or that the situations which they seek to make sense of lend themselves to induction in any case. These are scenarios which social workers typically face – where either there are competing accounts which need to be decided between, or where action needs to be taken in the here and now, which has implications for the future, on the basis of what has gone before (e.g. risk assessment). Decisions need to be made, and action must follow. These may appear logically correct, but nevertheless poor outcomes may result. This is because knowledge – despite associated aspirations – cannot guarantee to eliminate uncertainty.

Problems of positivism

The 'natural' and the 'social'

There is an enduring debate about the extent to which, given their different subject matter, it is appropriate to assume that the methods of natural science can be applied in non-scientific disciplines, especially the social sciences. 'Anti-naturalists' argue that they do not translate, given the contingent, contextual historicism of social phenomena. These also have a degree of complexity which makes the controlled experiments of the laboratory especially difficult to replicate, not least because of the influence of human psychology. In natural science, laws have particular value in aiding prediction, but in the social world this is more difficult, given this complexity but also the capacity of subjects to respond interactively. Attempts to specify relationships between variables are therefore inherently vulnerable to changes at either end of this continuum. Objectivity, meanwhile, is much more difficult, given the potential for allegiances and disagreements between researchers and researched, which make notions of neutrality harder to defend. Social science is therefore much more likely to concern itself with meaning than causation.

This status of scientific method as exemplar for knowledge production across the disciplines relates to Popper's claims that the practices of scientific practitioners are distinct from their traditional representation. The actual 'method' of science is best seen as one entailing trial and error. Hypotheses are inherently fallible, but much can be gained from their falsification. The process is ongoing, and the failure of one particular perspective does not challenge this progressive trajectory, rather it strengthens it. It is indeed therefore possible to specify particular variable relationships in the social world, and to develop knowledge in this fashion. Popper also suggested that although experimentation is central to science, there are scenarios which do not lend themselves to this methodology, and so often natural scientists will engage in imaginative speculative prediction – or 'thought experiments' – as a basis for filling in the gaps. As such, distinctions between the natural and social sciences are diminished.

Generalization

The 'problem of induction' – or generalization – represents an entire sub-discipline within the philosophy of science. It is concerned with the criteria which justify the extrapolation of what we know on the basis of previous experience to current or future scenarios – akin to risk assessment in social work. It arises because of concerns that knowledge claims derived from inductive reasoning are not as certain as those derived deductively. This is because it is not possible to observe or experience all instances of a phenomenon, and therefore there is always the possibility that a theory or knowledge claim is wrong. Popper suggested that the inherent uncertainty within inductively derived knowledge best be addressed by moving the focus of testing away from verification to falsification. Rather than asking whether or not a particular theory is true, and thus generalizable through law-like statements or rules, the question should be 'can we demonstrate that this theory is false?' Thus, hypotheses should still be tested, but it is falsification which is central to scientific method, not verification. A theory which is tested and appears to be true should be re-tested. Where a theory is shown to be untrue – that is, there are exceptions to its generality – falsification represents progress. In this way, observations and experiments represent the building blocks of theory. This view has been characterized by critics as naive empiricism, which fails to acknowledge the 'theory ladenness' of even those approaches to research which claim objectivity and neutrality as defining characteristics. Put another way, it is rare for a scientific researcher to approach a problem without prior immersion in the field, and complete objectivity would require that somehow this immersion had no effect upon the process of research or the analysis of research data. Many commentators claim that this is not possible, particularly in relation to the study of human beings by other human beings, and so induction should not be seen as inferior to deduction, nor objectivity reified at the expense of subjectivity.

The 'decline' of positivism

The decline of positivism as orthodoxy within science (and social science), then, and its replacement with some variations of alternative paradigmatic positions arose by virtue of both internal and external critique and development. Delanty and Strydom (2003) identify four major changes in ways of thinking about science and knowledge – epistemic shifts – which contributed to this decline. The 'logical turn' involved the overthrow of inductive empiricism by deductive reasoning within both the natural and social sciences. The 'linguistic turn' entailed the replacement of the primacy of the correspondence theory of truth, whereby knowledge is seen as a true representation of reality, with a form of ontological relativism. Consequently the dominance of science waned and was superseded by linguistic considerations. Knowledge came to be seen as constituted in and through language. These perspectives became more dominant over time, presaging the third, 'cultural historical turn', in which linguistic considerations became central to a fourth, much broader shift in which, following Kuhn, relativist views of the status of science assumed significance and knowledge came to be regarded as a social and historical construction. Cumulatively these confirm 'the crisis of the possibility of grounding social science on epistemic foundations' (2003: 9).

Post-positivism

In light of such developments, few hold true to the philosophy and methods of pure positivism any longer. Its flaws and limitations are evident. However, its principles and ethos inform 'post-positivist' viewpoints. Post-positivists hold to an ontologically realist position, but are epistemologically less certain. Thus, they believe that there is a 'real world' which is separate from our perceptions and constructions, but that objectivist assumptions about our ability to 'know' this world without our existing values or beliefs coming into play are not tenable. Reality is therefore seen as 'something that cannot be fully understood but it can be approximated' (Corby 2006: 49). It might not be possible to understand reality fully, but we can have confidence in efforts at approximation. Sometimes, the extent to which contemporary experimental research conducted in the positivist tradition has adapted to accommodate aspects of this critique is not acknowledged by proponents of alternative perspectives (Munro 1998).

Having discussed the development, characteristics and limitations of positivism at some length, it is now necessary to pay some attention to alternative paradigmatic positions.

Interpretivism

Interpretivism is often portrayed as standing in opposition to positivism. Thus, ontologically, interpretivism assumes human behaviour is deliberate and productive, understandable but not generalizable, and that knowledge arises through processes of communication and interpretation, with particular experiences having alternative meanings for different people. Rather than assuming that the process of producing knowledge should be value (or bias) free, interpretivists argue that it is not actually possible to 'bracket off' our beliefs and orientations in the manner which positivism suggests.

Interpretivists, then, do not believe that when it comes to the 'social' world, there is a single, fixed 'reality' out there which we can unproblematically investigate and know without the mediation of our values and beliefs, which in any case inter-relate with the meanings and interpretations of others. Instead, there are multiple truths. The separation of the observer from the subject – an essential requirement of objectivity under positivism – is not tenable, and so the necessity of pursuing truth through scientific method is redundant, opening up space for methods which better reflect the assumption that reality is inter-subjectively constructed. The suggestion is that it is not possible to study the social world using the methods employed in the natural sciences, given their respective positions regarding the nature of subjectivity. Humans bring their subjective perceptions to the table, and so there is emphasis on interpretation as the principal means of gaining understanding. Knowledge is not waiting to be discovered but created through experience. The various interpretive traditions, including phenomenology, ethnomethodology, symbolic interactionism, social constructionism and post-modernism seek to use individual subjectivities as a basis for theorizing the changing nature of the world and our interaction with it. Language plays a significant constituting role in 'making up' reality as it is perceived and experienced by individuals.

Limitations of interpretivism

Though interpretivism is arguably the dominant paradigm within contemporary social science, it has been subject to strong criticism, particularly with regard to its inherent relativism. Hammersley sums up the implications: 'The problem of the self-refuting character of relativism is well known: in claiming that all truth is relative to a framework, it makes its own truth relative, and thus false in terms of other frameworks even from the point of view of relativism itself' (1995: 107). Knowledge claims made within this tradition are therefore vulnerable to the accusation that there are no criteria via which these truth claims can be assessed, and so no basis on which to determine whether a claim should be attributed the status of knowledge, opinion of belief. Relativism is self refuting: 'if relativism is true, then the statement 'relativism is true' is no more true than the statement 'relativism is false'. This leads to the conclusion that relativism cannot be true' (Mantysaari 2005: 94).

Critical theory

Many of the perspectives which are held dear in social work, not least anti-oppressive practice, and critical and transformative 'varieties' of practice have their roots in this paradigm. Critical theory is associated with the work of many key thinkers in the history and development of social science, including Karl Marx, the 'Frankfurt' school, and Jürgen Habermas. A key proposition within much critical theorizing is that human experience and behaviour is delimited, influenced or constrained by structural considerations and social divisions.

Those who are influenced by critical theory are concerned with the impact which social structures have upon individuals, particularly those who experience discrimination and disadvantage as a result. The view here is that the lives and behaviours – the subjective experiences – of individuals are shaped by an objective reality, which has constituting, meaningful and often negative effects. The assumption is that embedded within the experiences of the oppressed is a more complete knowledge, which is often suppressed but which is actually key to understanding the nature of reality. As such, there are affiliations with so-called 'standpoint' perspectives which generally seek to bring to the fore knowledge which is often disregarded within dominant discourses.

Arguably, critical theory represents a paradigm in its own right, though its distinctive ontological and epistemological positions overlap with other paradigms. It shares with interpretivism the assumption that the nature of reality (the meaning of experience) is interpreted and experienced differently, though its goals are collective rather than individualized. Causal laws which represent the basis of categorizations and classifications are viewed as flawed by virtue of their neglect of the 'voices' of the oppressed. However the impact of social structure is regarded as being real, with constituting effects, and so there is overlap with positivism. Objectivity and subjectivity merge in the critical approach, in that as individuals we are created by the world in which we live, but by the meanings we make of our experience and the decisions and actions which follow, we also have effect on that world. This in essence is the position taken by Giddens (1984) in delineating the mechanisms of structuration as a means of resolving the structure–agency debate. Traditional notions of scientific expertise are rejected. Though there is a strong alignment to value driven commitments, there is also a genuine concern to better understand the mechanisms via which society functions, particularly the interplay between wider structure, individual meaning and group conflict and consensus, which arguably mitigates unfettered ideology. In this respect, there are links with realism.

The limitations of critical theory reflect its particular positioning, which render it vulnerable to accusations of bias. We explore these in some depth in Chapter 4.

Realism

Is it possible to reconcile positivism with interpretive and critical paradigms, given the relativity inherent within the former and the clear subjective, value driven, nature of the latter? Realism offers some potential here, as it draws upon aspects of both positivist and interpretivist thought, and itself takes a 'critical' stance.

There are varieties of realism. Blaikie (2007), for example, refers to 'shallow', 'conceptual', 'cautious', 'depth', 'idealist' and 'subtle' versions, while Kazi (2003) adds 'transcendental', 'referential' and 'fallibilistic'. Despite their variety, at heart these alternatives are based upon shared ontological and epistemological propositions.

Realism represents a significant challenge to the dominance of positivist and interpretivist positions within the social sciences. Scientific realists argue strongly that there is a world beyond the impressions that we carry in our minds, and that we can come to know the world in a way which bears some resemblance to its true nature, though by no means infallibly. Its challenge to positivism stems from its rejection of the notion that it is only observable phenomena which are amenable to 'capture' via scientific method, broadening out this focus to encompass unobserved phenomena. The suggestion is that realism 'takes seriously the existence of the things, structures and mechanisms revealed by the sciences at different levels of reality' (Houston 2005: 13). Ontologically, then, its position is at odds with the focus on 'multiple truths' in interpretivism, and more closely aligned with positivist assumptions. Epistemologically, experience is the principal means via which we come to know the world in which we live, but has its own limitations.

'Critical' realism is perhaps the most influential 'form' of realism in the social sciences. It derives from the influential writings of the philosopher of science, Roy Bhaskar (e.g. 1997). It is at the level of causation that critical realism is distinctive. He suggested that we can infer the existence of relationships between variables – causal mechanisms – via the presence of phenomena. We do not need to observe a phenomenon to 'know' that it has had an effect and therefore must 'exist'. Gravity is a good example. Thus, although ontologically, there are shared assumptions here with positivism, this is a very different way of thinking about how we might know the world – epistemology – than that which is assumed by empiricists or interpretivists. The focus shifts from a conceptualization of knowledge as an understanding of the nature of the relationship between variables established via observing their operation in practice, to one in which witnessing a particular phenomena points us to the existence and operation of causal mechanisms. A new arena for enquiry also opens up – the investigation, understanding and explanation of 'unseen' causal mechanisms.

Bhaskar's critical orientation opens up scope for integration with critical and emancipatory theory and practice – and thus for rapprochement of positivism, interpretivism and critical perspectives. Critical realism rejects the positivist commitment to value neutrality in the production of knowledge. At the same time, however, there is recognition that the experience of oppression is variable – that is, there are multiple truths, also the interpretive position.

Realism 'works' retroductively rather than inductively or deductively. This entails the identification of patterns, followed by the generation of hypotheses which seek to account for their existence in terms of underlying mechanisms. These hypotheses are then analysed for the adequacy of their explanation on the basis of evidence which points to credibility. The assumption is that simplistic explanations are likely to be inadequate unless they accommodate the capacity for interaction between mechanisms operating at different levels of reality within open systems (such as social, psychological and biological) as well as the variable degrees of agency which individuals concerned are likely to possess. The fact that mechanisms may operate in opposition to each other helps to account for the variable effects they have in individual cases. However, whereas the strict application of hypothetico-deductive method would seek to establish the direct relationship between variables, mechanisms and outcomes, here there is recognition of the inherent difficulties in doing so (Houston 2005). This realization means that the difference between reality and how we represent it is taken seriously. The implicit belief in the inadequacy of explanatory power contributes to the generation of alternative hypotheses in a cyclical process which lends itself to the systematic accumulation of both data and evidence.

Certain implications for social science (and social work) flow from this perspective. Emphasis is placed on the significance of the system, or context, within which mechanisms are operating, for properly understanding their working. Although we might be able to reach an explanation or understanding of the operation of mechanisms in systems, our finding in one system will not be transferable to alternative contexts, because the various mechanisms of which each is comprised are distinctive and the interactions between them unique. Realists may therefore refer to tendencies, but nothing more. In social science, the structure–agency debate – concerned with the extent to which our actions are voluntary or determined by social structure –

will be enduring, as where the line is drawn will depend upon very particular factors that cannot be extrapolated deterministically. In social work, this means: 'we can never predict the outcome of any intervention' (Houston 2001: 850) with any particular degree of confidence. Where it is possible to understand and specify the relationship between variables and outcomes, such explanations are contextually specific. It is therefore acknowledged that the focus for investigation is context–mechanism interactions in situated contexts. Although it is possible to 'know' about the world, this knowledge is not necessarily applicable to other 'parts' of the world. Though the world is real, we cannot know it fully.

For different reasons, then, both realists and interpretivists focus their investigations on localized phenomena, without aspiring to the development of predictions and causal laws, as under positivism. Realism thus offers a bridge between positivism and interpretivism by virtue of its simultaneous recognition of the veracity of the relativist claim that knowledge is context dependent, but also that it represents some approximation of the reality of the world in which we live. This link stems from realism's acknowledgement that although there is a real world, non-'real' mechanisms – such as language – can have constituting effect, and thus methods associated with interpretivist perspectives can be usefully employed by realists, even though, ontologically, interpretivists make different assumptions. The emphasis on 'tendencies' points to the accommodation of the reciprocal significance of individual agency in social contexts, which is a concern shared with interpretivists. Similarly, although realists are sceptical regarding the positivist assertion of necessary correspondence between 'truth' and 'reality', they are less enamoured of notions of 'multiple truths', preferring the notion of 'a single truth in each of many and varied contexts'. Although realists are committed to the idea that what we perceive of as reality has substance, they also recognize 'human actions are concept-dependant, and human concepts make up a part of the reality of these facts' (Kazi 2003: 60). Despite these affinities, however, realists also acknowledge the limitations of an approach to understanding life which is over reliant on discursive aspects of the world. Thus, there are similarities to scientific method, properly understood, in that there is recognition that because our explanations of mechanism–context interactions are contextually specific, we can never have a full, true account of reality. Instead, realists are aware of the limitations of their partial, 'best fit' and inherently revisable knowledge claims and the role that falsification may play in theory development.

Limitations of realism

There are various challenges to the scientific realist position. Perhaps the hardest argument for realists to refute fully relates to the nature of progress and discovery. Theories represent current, 'state of the art' thinking regarding the nature of phenomena, their effects, and what is likely to occur in the future. They are supported by evidence testifying to their accuracy. However, they have superseded previously existing theories which themselves were taken to represent the pinnacle of progress. If those preceding theories have been shown to be false in the process of being superseded by contemporary knowledge, and they in turn superseded theories which existed before them, *ad infinitum*, then on what basis should we have faith in contemporary theories? Are they not likely to be superseded too?

Realists argue that such arguments are flawed in their assumption that all previous theories have been superseded. The notion of a paradigm shift is significant here whereby all that has gone before is superseded by new, superior assumptions. But paradigm 'shifts' are metaphorical – a means of enabling us to represent historical fluctuations in dominant ideas, rather than 'real' events. Some theories may have been replaced, but others remain influential – they stand the test of time.

Additionally, it may also be the case that what is at issue here is not the nature of reality, but the status we ascribe to method as a basis for ascribing value, namely empiricism. Sometimes, competing theories will all be underpinned by evidence, and so deciding which is correct, adequate or true becomes problematic, even within science. Here, the suggestion is that 'by evidence alone we cannot tell whether a theory is true. All we can establish...is whether the theory is empirically adequate' (Bortolotti 2008: 100). Thus, in deciding between competing accounts, something other than empirical evidence will need to be used as a determining criterion. One suggestion is that of overall coherence with our existing wider theoretical framework. Empirical adequacy becomes the benchmark which determines the success or failure of a hypothesis. This is unrelated to knowledge or truth, which are external concerns. Similarly, it has been suggested that what determines a choice between competing theories is scientific pragmatism. In social work, for example, there are competing explanations of mental disorder, the cognitive and the psychodynamic. Neither meets the claim of empirical adequacy, and so the decision with regard to which represents the best 'fit' with the reality of mental illness is made on the basis of alternative criteria which we have separate, non-empirical, reasons to prefer. Although a theory may have been shown to be inaccurate, we therefore understand why nevertheless it was adequate. Empirical method captures not the nature of reality, but the nature of the relations between variables which help to constitute reality.

These positions are taken to undermine positivism, but do not necessarily undermine realism, because it is inherent within realism that there are limits to what can be known about the nature of the world via empirical methods, which seek to isolate and thus specify the relationships between variables. Realism retains merit as an alternative means of gradually filtering and refining what we know.

Exercise

With regard to each of the four distinctive paradigms we have specified:

what does each assume about, firstly, the nature of reality, and secondly, how we might know this?

'Ways of knowing'

We have elaborated the key characteristics and criticisms of major paradigmatic positions. What should be apparent by now is that these represent very different ways of thinking about the nature of the world and how we might come better to understand. Each paradigm takes a particular ontological and epistemological position. Epistemologically, positivism and realism are broadly realist, though with subtle distinctions (realism being 'post-positivist') while both interpretivism and critical theory (though this is problematic for the latter) lean towards constructivism, or what Blaikie refers to as 'anti-foundationalism – 'there are no permanent, unvarying criteria for establishing whether knowledge can be regarded as true, and there are no absolute truths' (2007: 23).

Different paradigms, then, represent alternative 'ways of knowing'. As Everitt et al. put it 'Different ways of knowing...the world make different assumptions about the individual and society and their inter-relationship' (1992: 135). In other words, alternative paradigms are incompatible. Each implies alternative formulations of ontological and epistemological assumptions. According to Kuhn, because of these differing underpinning assumptions, paradigmatic positions are rendered incommensurate, meaning it is not possible to believe in more than one position at the same time. This has significant implications for how knowledge generated within distinctive traditions might be used within alternative frameworks.

Knowledge in social work

Discussion of paradigms, their underpinning assumptions and defining characteristics and the potential incompatibilities which flow from these demonstrate why it might be that the nature and status of knowledge is contested. They provide a necessary contextual backdrop without which the discussion of the nature or types of knowledge in social work would be diminished. However, they also problematize efforts to formulate precise and predictable solutions to specific problems – arguably, the *raison d'etre* of social work. Given that knowledge is so contested and tenuous, how can we go forward? In order to answer this question we need to explore debates about the nature of knowledge in social work, and the relationship between knowledge and practice.

Knowledge for what?

The nature of the social work enterprise is also contested. There are ongoing debates concerning what social work 'is' or 'should' be and how best it should achieve its aims. These debates are long-standing. It is nevertheless possible to identify points on which there is consensus and thus identify key activities in which all social workers are involved to some extent.

Firstly, social work encompasses a plethora of related but distinct activities, held together by a general commitment to ensuring that concerns about individual welfare are not neglected in societal responses to social problems, and its objectives and methods reflect this. There is general agreement that the stakes are high in social work, with potentially serious implications flowing from whether or not practitioners are involved in the lives of service users, and what they do when they are. Decision-making and action – or, as they tend to be referred to, assessment and intervention – universally represent the means via which practitioners seek to have an effect. The fact that these activities form the basis on which the entire social work enterprise is founded has implications for our discussion of social work knowledge, as the use to which knowledge is put by practitioners is determined by their activities. The question then arises, how can practitioners make decisions and act with confidence where knowledge is contested?

'Forms' of knowledge in social work

Knowledge is a key component in the definition of professionalism. Professional competence is comprised of three complementary strands – skills, values and knowledge. It also contributes to the delineation of the focus of a particular profession, helping to define it and differentiate it from others. The professional status of social work is precarious, not least because there is a lack of clarity regarding 'what constitutes the *knowledge base of social work* and how this can be applied to the dilemmas regularly encountered' in practice (Trevithnick 2008: 1212).

In the absence of consensus with regard to how knowledge should be constituted, there is some agreement that whatever knowledge may be, it takes various forms – as Sheppard puts it: 'the rather startling truth is that there are indeed different types or forms of knowledge' (2004: 42). Various typologies have been developed, which differentiate between knowledge types and knowledge sources (Pawson et al. 2003; Trevithnick 2008). The former might include the distinctions between knowing the factual basis of a subject or discipline in depth as opposed to having the skills to be able to achieve a particular end. The latter includes tradition, authority, and experience, themselves varying according to the position and purpose of the stakeholder grouping from which they emerge.

It is helpful to differentiate between empirics, aesthetics, personal experience and ethics as all contributing to the knowledge base for practice. Empirical knowledge is that which is based upon scientific studies, intended to describe, explain or predict social processes and behaviour. Aesthetics is more concerned with those aspects of practice which are sometimes characterized as 'artistic' rather than 'scientific', including interpersonal work and engagement. Personal knowledge is concerned with drawing on our inherent personal experience, and the knowledge which results from this, in work with others. Ethics, though seen as representing a form of bias by some, 'contaminating' the knowledge production process, is central to social work's commitment to social justice and thus to defining the objectives of practice and seeking to achieve these. Ethics, then, do (and according to some, *cannot not*) inform practice-based decision-making. As should be apparent, empirical knowledge can be equated with positivism, aesthetics and personal knowledge with interpretivism, and ethical knowledge with critical theory.

The knowledge base of social work, then, is seen by some as necessarily encompassing all of these forms of knowledge (Wilson et al. 2008). Although empirics is privileged by some by virtue of its close correspondence with the assumptions and methods of science, in practice settings it is not necessarily the status of knowledge but its utility which is paramount. For this reason, some place equal emphasis on the 'artistic' aspects of practice, and its ethical underpinnings. There are tensions here, which we elaborate on in Chapter 7.

Often in practice-based disciplines a distinction is drawn between knowing *that* and knowing *how*, where the former refers to the theoretical basis of a discipline and the latter to the ability to utilize this knowledge in securing particular aims in practice. The knowledge developed and 'held' by practitioners, drawn from their experience of applying theory or knowledge, is arguably distinct from more formalized facts or theory. Its application is dependent on some degree of intuitive understanding and ability informed by tacit knowledge. This distinction reflects a tension between formal theoretical or propositional knowledge and informal practical or experiential knowledge – or between what Trevithnick refers to as 'a more scientific, technical-rational and expert-orientated approach to knowledge' (2008: 1215) and professional, process or action knowledge.

The first of these privileges rationality, generalizability and similar 'scientific' and 'formal' principles as the basis for practice. This is potentially problematic as the privileging of certain varieties of knowledge results in generalized rules which often do not apply straightforwardly in complex practice scenarios. The suggestion is that these difficulties can be remedied by the use of different 'forms' of knowledge in an integrative and complementary, rather than isolated, fashion. This enables integration between what is known and what needs to be known. 'Process' knowledge emphasizes that knowledge cannot be applied without amendment to suit the context in which it is used. 'Action' knowledge emphasizes that the application of knowledge in practice settings is dependent on, and should not be seen as something separate from, the skills and techniques which are required to 'make knowledge work' in practice. Healy (2005) similarly points to the ways in which the context in which knowledge is applied and the nature of that knowledge interact reciprocally.

There have been fluctuations between the relative positioning of each over time and – depending on your perspective – either a decline in the prominence of scientific theoretical knowledge and consequent rise to prominence of experiential knowledge, or, with the recent emphasis on evidence-based practice, a decline in the significance accorded to intuitive capacities in favour of formalized (and formulaic) knowledge. There is no intrinsic need, however, to view this debate in 'either/or' terms, as in practice there is scope for integrating analytic and intuitive knowledge, which continually interweave in a dynamic fashion.

These are complex debates, which are not easily resolvable, as demonstrated by their enduring character. Shaw (1999) draws attention to the potentially paralysing effect of too much philosophical and methodological discussion. In such circumstances, a more pragmatic approach is advocated, whereby the need for knowledge to be adapted for use in practice is acknowledged. This is a 'fallible realist' or 'weak constructionist' position, which acknowledges that knowledge and truth cannot be neatly equated and thus the status of knowledge for practice cannot be assumed but is nevertheless substantive.

'Types' of knowledge in social work

Exercise

Think about social work. Whose views and perspectives should be taken into account in making decisions about if and how to intervene? What is distinctive about what these individuals or groups might know which will be useful in such scenarios?

Debates about knowledge in social work, then, reflect wider debates within the philosophy of knowledge which, though more long-standing, are also far from closure. Your own view on these debates will no doubt in turn reflect your particular worldview, and the paradigmatic assumptions embedded within this. Alternatively, you might take a resolutely pragmatic stance whereby the usefulness of knowledge for practice reflects its utility to the task or problem with which you are faced. If so, perhaps unwittingly, your views reflect another philosophical position, pragmatism. We will discuss the role that some form of realistic pragmatism might play as a basis for rapprochement between competing perspectives in the conclusion.

Coincidentally, a pragmatic stance is also taken by SCIE in an influential attempt to develop a classificatory framework for understanding knowledge in social work (Pawson et al. 2003). This represents a significant intervention in debates about forms of knowledge in practice. The intention was to render contested knowledge 'useable' by practitioners in a context in which there were concerns that advocates of 'strong' versions of knowledge-based practice disregarded the potentially significant contribution to practice made by informal, tacit and experiential knowledge. SCIE sought better to ensure that practice was knowledge based while also doing justice to the role of alternative forms and sources of knowledge, by developing guidance on how practitioners might assess the status and usefulness of knowledge claims depending on their 'source'. Their typology refers to knowledge held by practitioners, the policy community, service users and carers, researchers and organizations, and specified criteria for assessing knowledge quality according to the acronym 'TAPUPAS'. Here, transparency, accuracy, propriety, utility, accessibility and specificity are taken as determining the status which is attached to a knowledge claim within a particular context.

Arguably, SCIE is taking a position here which sets it against advocates of evidence-based practice premised upon a 'hierarchy of knowledge'. Whereas informal, tacit knowledge is seen as not meeting the criteria for knowledge in 'pure' knowledge-based practice, Fisher (2002) believes that the development of a broad knowledge base for practice must include such knowledge. The analogy of 'a framework, rather than a straitjacket' is used, in which all forms of knowledge can play a part in practice. This is seen as more relevant and realistic, given the nature of social work 'on the ground'.

It would be a mistake to take SCIE's review as either a definitive or final resolution – not least because it was intended as a starting point in an ongoing process. Various criticisms have been leveled against the typology. Wilson et al., for example, criticize the framework for utilizing a conceptualization of 'theory' which, despite its rhetoric, is nevertheless broadly formal, doing detriment to informal knowledge sources. SCIE's sources are seen as 'externally created and do not arise from personal practice-related experiences' (2008: 110). Shaw (2008: 190) meanwhile suggests that 'there may be as much diversity of knowledge by acquaintance and description *within* each of these as there is *between* them' which makes the application of evaluative criteria in any consistent manner problematic. Nevertheless, SCIE's taxonomy represents an authoritative 'take' on how social work as a whole can progress such debates, rather than remaining mired in complex and sometimes esoteric theoretical discussions about how we can best understand the nature and consequences of the relationship between knowledge, practice and outcomes. We turn our attention to this task in the chapters which follow, using SCIE's typology of knowledge 'sources' as a basis for more specific discussion of the issues raised in this chapter.

2

Intervention: Does it Work? Research, Evidence and Evidence-Based Practice

This chapter examines ideas about effective social work practice as they have crystallized around the idea of evidence-based practice. The notion that social work practice should be guided by good-quality evidence seems self-evident. How can one argue against the idea that practice should be based on evidence? However, on closer examination, the idea throws up a series of fundamental questions. Evidence is the basis of good practice – but what is 'evidence'? Is there only one source of evidence? Or are there multiple sources? Research findings, for instance, are an important source; but what about practice experience, theory and ideas? If there are multiple sources of evidence, what is the relationship between them?

Take the example of a woman who expresses concern about her eighty-year-old mother, who has started to do forgetful things, such as leave her keys in the door and leave the cooker on, unattended. The daughter feels that her mother should go into care; but her mother insists that there is no serious problem. The GP's diagnosis is inconclusive. Research articles describe the early symptoms of dementia – but do they apply in this case? Furthermore, this morning you realized on your way to work that you'd left the grill on. All this information is appropriate; but someone needs to weigh it up and make a judgement.

And what about the very definition of evidence: evidence of what, and for what purpose? What is the difference between good and bad evidence? Finally, how does the idea of evidence relate to the nature of practice and the larger role of the practitioner? In this chapter we will consider these questions by looking at the idea of evidence-based practice (EBP) and its application to social work.

Evidence, in the sense of empirical research which can inform practice, has a long-standing pedigree in social work. The work of Reid, for instance, in relation to the development of task-centred social work, is an example of this (Shaw 2004). However, the idea of EBP is a specific version of the idea that practice should be informed by empirical research, which looks to the evidence-based practice movement in medicine as the model for developing social work practice. Work in Britain is seen as a leading element of EBP in social work (Gray and MacDonald 2006); so this chapter will primarily draw on the work of the key exponents of this movement in Britain to present the approach.

Before looking in detail at how EBP has been applied in social work, it is necessary to understand this approach in medicine. This has the added value for social workers of also enabling them to understand an important influence in the practice of fellow professionals in the multi-disciplinary teams that now characterize the working environment for many social work professionals.

A preliminary point that it is also necessary to make is that, in talking about evidence-based practice here, we will be distinguishing its original form, in medicine – to which we will refer by the acronym EBM (evidence-based medicine) – from its translation into social work, to which we will refer as EBSW (evidence-based social work). This distinction, you will see as the chapter progresses, is important, because it enables us to consider not only what EBM has to offer social work, but also to compare and contrast its approach with that of EBSW.

Evidence-based medicine

Evidence-based practice in medicine developed to address a perceived problem in traditional medical practice, namely excessive reliance on the authority of teachers, texts and hierarchical superiors rather than the practitioner's own informed and independent judgement (EBMWG: 1992). It also seeks to enable medical practice to access and evaluate up-to-date research – from the natural sciences and applied medical studies – relevant to day-to-day practice (Davidoff et al. 1995). A particularly influential aspect of evidence-based medicine (EBM) has been its focus on the use and critical evaluation of research in practice. In short, EBM has sought to help medical practice incorporate external evidence with the existing skills of medical practice; and enable practitioners to use rules of evidence to assess the quality of research (EBMWG 1992; Sackett et al. 1996).

EBM was developed to complement and enhance, rather than replace, the use of clinical experience, intuition and theory. Research enables practitioners to put their practice experience and intuition within a broader frame of reference and to think critically and systematically about their experience. Research also helps practitioners to reflect critically on the 'facts' and theories – about the cause, progress and treatment of disease – that they may take for granted. Nevertheless, EBM values the thoughtful use of clinical experience and theory. Clinical experience has a central role in developing the judgement needed to understand the patient's problem. It also plays an important part in identifying relevant research; and in making decisions about how to employ research in treatment: 'Clinical experience and the development of clinical instincts (particularly with respect to diagnosis) are crucial... [as] many aspects of clinical practice cannot, or will not, ever be adequately tested' (EBMWG 1992: 2421). Theory is also important in evidence-based practice – evidence does not exist in a vacuum. Research tests ideas and hunches that come from theories, and to understand what the 'facts' are saying, it's necessary to understand the theory. Theory enables practitioners to interpret and make sense of research findings. It also fills in the gaps in knowledge that are widespread because of 'the dearth of adequate evidence.' (EBMWG 1992: 2423)

As potential patients we find reassuring the critical prod that EBM provides to good medicine practice. Furthermore, it would be churlish to dismiss any lessons it has to offer social work as a profession simply because these ideas come from medical education and practice. Social work, we should remember, has a long history of borrowing good ideas from medical practice – such as the idea of 'defensive practice' (Harris 1987). However, it would also be misguided simply to transfer ideas from medicine to social work without considering the differences and similarities of practice in these two disciplines.

In social work, as in medicine, we deal with people who have complex problems, and we have to employ a range of information sources to decide how best to address those problems. At a basic level, then, there is a sufficient similarity in medicine and social work as helping professions, to support the relevance of evidence-based practice in medicine to social work in terms of its concern that up-to-date good-quality external evidence is incorporated into practice decision-making. Decision-making in both professions involves combining and balancing evidence from a range of sources, and here EBM seems to offer a useful framework within which to consider the use of different sources of knowledge and how they interact.

However, there are also clear differences between the two professions, and any application of the principles of EBM to social work needs to take account of these differences. The two disciplines have different foci in their work with people, and different bodies of research knowledge to inform their practice. The focus, but not the exclusive concern, of medicine is the physical, biochemical aspects of people (General Medical Council 2003). Medicine is also concerned with the psychology and social aspects of people, but these are not its focus. Social work, on the other hand, is primarily concerned with people as agents, with their own histories, who are acting in the context of complex social forces that both enable and constrain them. Again, this is a focus that does not exclude an overlap with other disciplines, such as psychology and law (TOPSS 2002). But these very different foci of concern underline the different skills and forms of knowledge on which the disciplines draw to inform and guide their day-to-day practice (see Box 2.1 on p. 44).

In outlining the approach of EBM, our concern has been to present an approach which has been influential in medical practice and across disciplines allied to Health and Social Care (Newman et al. 2005). It has not been possible here to explore the arguments about evidence-based practice in medicine itself; all we can do is note that it is not an uncontentious approach (e.g. Williams and Gardner 2002). As mentioned above, EBM has been influential across Health and Social Care professions, and in the remainder of this chapter we want to consider how this approach has been applied to social work and social care. This approach – evidence-based social work, preceded by 'regularly changing brand names' (Sheldon and Macdonald 2008: 66) – is particularly associated in Britain with the work of Brian Sheldon and Geraldine Macdonald and, accordingly we will draw primarily on their accounts and arguments.

Evidence-based social work

In this section we will look at how EBM has been translated into social work. We will focus on two key issues. The first is how EBSW has applied evidence-based medicine's emphasis on the use of research to inform practice in terms of the critical interplay of research evidence, clinical judgement and theory. Second, we will consider the

---

Box 2.1   What Social Workers and Doctors Need to Know

Social Workers
Social workers must:

a. Have knowledge of:
    - services relevant to individuals', carers', families', groups' and communities' needs and circumstances (not just those offered by their organisation) and how to access other relevant services
    - benefits and direct payments
    - legislation
b. Have in-depth knowledge of the individuals, families, carers, groups and communities group they are working with.

(TOPSS 2002: para. 5)

Doctors
Graduates must have a knowledge and understanding of the clinical and basic sciences. They must also understand relevant parts of the behavioural and social sciences, and be able to integrate and critically evaluate evidence from all these sources to provide a firm foundation for medical practice.

They must know about and understand normal and abnormal structure and function, including the natural history of human diseases, the body's defence mechanisms, disease presentation and responses to illness. This will include an understanding of the genetic, social and environmental factors that determine disease and the response to treatment.

(General Medical Council 2003: paras. 13–14)

---

appropriateness of the ideas of good-quality evidence that EBSW has imported into social work from medicine.

Research, judgement and theory – evidence in practice?

There are good reasons to think that evidence-based medicine can make an important and stimulating contribution to discussions within social work about the relationship of research evidence to practice, and how practice knowledge, intuition and theory provide evidence for practice decision-making. However, when we look at EBSW, it has clearly experienced problems in translating EBM's commitment to practice skills and theoretical knowledge, as well as research, into its approach to social work. Sheldon and MacDonald, for instance, formulate their own definition of EBSW as follows:

Evidence-based social care is the conscientious, explicit and judicious use of current best evidence in making decisions regarding the welfare of individuals, groups and communities. (Sheldon and Macdonald 2008:68)

However, their account of evidence-based practice has a much more truncated sense of evidence than that given by a leading text on 'Evidence-Based Medicine' (Strauss et al. 2005), which emphasizes practice wisdom alongside research evidence and the perspective of users.

Evidence-based medicine requires the integration of the best research evidence with our clinical expertise and our patient's unique values and circumstances. (ibid.: 1)

Sheldon and Macdonald play down the role of professional judgement in terms of practice knowledge and intuition, as can be seen when they expand on and explain their definition of EBSW. They explain that: 'conscientious*ness*' relates to the ethical obligation ensuring that practice is informed by the most up-to-date and best-quality research; '*explicitness*' entails clarity of assessment, identifying clear, specifiable options and relating these to what is known about their effectiveness; and '*judiciousness*' is sound judgement. However, they add: 'Our stock...is not high in this matter, and considered pragmatism has been out of fashion for three decades at least. We seem, lacking a healthy professional immune system, to be prone to infection by fads and fashions' (Sheldon and Macdonald 2008: 71). A less dismissive attitude towards practice expertise can be found in other accounts of EBSW – for instance, Newman et al. (2005).

The argument put forward for EBSW is that current social work is a problem – it is woolly minded and prone to bias – and that EBSW is the answer, both practically and ethically. Current social work practice – outside EBSW – may be well-intentioned but this does not prevent it being misguided and ill-informed about what works. EBSW is critical of what it sees as others' concern with: '...a shared, happy-clappy, non-discriminatory, non-post-code lottery, commitment to equal and speedy access to ineffective services' (Sheldon and Macdonald 2008: 68). Particular foci for criticisms are counselling and person-centred approaches, and radical social work. The influence of Carl Rodgers on social work (Sheldon and Macdonald 1999) and the impact of 'barefoot psychoanalysis in the 60s (in-depth relationships but not gas stoves...)' (Sheldon 2001: 803) particularly raises the hackles of EBSW. Radical social work is another target for criticism:

'...booing from the touchline but leading to no positive advice as to what we might actually do about child abuse or mental health care' (ibid.: 804). These problems, in the eyes of the proponents of EBSW, point to a deeper malaise in social work, which is a combination of a laissez-faire attitude to intervention – i.e. practitioners choose whichever approach they like, because all approaches are considered equally valid; and a belief that intuition and experience or a theory can provide as good a basis for decision-making in practice as research evidence.

EBSW's solution has two elements. The first element is ethical. Social work, it argues, should focus on 'what works' for service users (will an intervention achieve what it aims to achieve, with minimum adverse consequences?); and what works for the taxpayer (Hudson and Roberts 1998: 154; Newman et al. 2005). Furthermore, ethical questions should be addressed in terms more of empirical evaluation than of critical examination, principles and power. Social work, Macdonald argues, has: 'tended to be more concerned with larger questions of philosophy and ethics: whose rights and interest should be protected or have pre-eminence...These are certainly important concerns, but there should be a closer relationship between empirical questions and wider questions of "shoulds" and "oughts"' (Macdonald 1994: 405). To go back to the earlier example, of a forgetful mother and her concerned daughter: if the former insists that she is capable, and the latter that she needs full-time care, whose voice has greater weight, and how do you decide this? Does your own experience of having left the grill on colour your experience, and should it? Do you start from the assumption that older people will be forgetful, or that their forgetfulness is of a different quality from yours? Ethical issues are as essential as the facts.

The second element is a prescription of a generous dose of 'science' to 'immunize' staff against famous ideas and famous names (Sheldon 2001, Sheldon and Macdonald 2008). Sheldon, for instance, argues that science will inject a healthy scepticism into social work, challenging biases arising from preference and ideological commitment. Furthermore, science provides the sort of research evidence that, EBSW thinks, will best answer questions about what works in social work (Sheldon 2001). EBSW sees social work practice in terms of distinct interventions, the social equivalent of drug treatment in medicine, and values evidence in relation to what it can tell social work about 'what sort of problems are amenable to what sorts of interventions, in what circumstance, and with what degree of certainty' (Macdonald 2001). In line with this view EBSW sees the criteria of good evidence in medicine as directly applicable to social work. The key message here of EBSW is that:

> When studying the effects of interventions we must learn to live with a hierarchy of research methods and attributive confidence, for only experimental, or at a push, comparative approaches, have the bias-reduction properties to encourage us to head off in one direction rather than another with any sense of security. (Sheldon and Macdonald 1999: 3)

In summary, EBSW puts forward a narrower version of evidence-based practice than in its medical counterpart. As originally developed in medicine, evidence-based practice entails balanced judgements based on external evidence from research and theory and internal evidence gathered through clinical experience. In EBSW, practice expertise and theory are treated with suspicion and downplayed. The nature of good decision-making in EBSW seems not to be the balanced dialogue of external and internal evidence put forward by EBM. Rather, it involves adopting an attitude of 'paranoia' (sic) about knowledge from sources other than 'scientific' research, which gives a pressing priority to external evidence (Sheldon 2001: 806).

Good evidence for good practice

EBSW is committed to rigorous research and emphasizes the need for practitioners to assess the quality of research and to understand its strengths and weaknesses. On this basis, qualitative as well as quantitative research has a role to play in EBSW. When, for instance, a practitioner wants to explore an issue – to work out what might be going on, why people are acting as they are – small-scale studies and qualitative research can provide insights, suggest options and help practitioners formulate hypotheses – hunches – to test (Thyer and Wodarski 1998; Newman et al. 2005).

However, when the focus moves to questions of the best course of action, the most effective and efficient intervention, EBSW argues that quantitative studies are superior because their design addresses problems of bias and generalizability(see Chapter 4). A particular concern of EBSW is to identify which interventions work, and to exclude from practice interventions that may be harmful. Here, it sees quantitative intervention studies as particularly important. Some forms of quantitative research are preferred to others, because they are more able

---

Box 2.2

Exercise
Evidence-based practice emphasizes the need to use critical skills in assessing research knowledge. The Centre for Evidence-Based Practice developed critical thinking tools for the analysis of research. Copies of these can be downloaded from: www.ripfa.org.uk/aboutus/archive/skills.asp? TOPcatsubID=4&id=4

- Obtain copies of the following: Bradshaw, W. (2003) 'Use of single-system research to evaluate the effectiveness of cognitive-behavioural treatment of schizophrenia' in *British Journal of Social Work* 33 (7): 885–99; and Kim, K. and Fox, M. (2006) 'Moving to a Holistic Model of Health among Persons with Mobility Disabilities' in *Qualitative Social Work* 5 (4): 470–88.
- Decide which critical thinking tools would be appropriate for evaluating these two pieces of research.
- Note how you choose which tool to use for which piece of research and then refer to the box at the end of this chapter.

---

to reduce bias, and identify with greater precision what was done and with what effect. This is the idea of a hierarchy of evidence: the idea that intervention studies can be sorted according to their power in identifying and specifying the effect of an intervention – their 'attributive confidence' (Sheldon and Macdonald 2008: 75–7).

Studies which look at a situation before and after an intervention – 'pre/post tests' – are helpful in identifying change. They do not necessarily show that the change arose from the intervention (what was done): it could have been the result of chance. According to EBSW, a better way of identifying change and what might have caused it is a quasi-experimental study, involving two or more groups of similar people who receive different interventions and (as in the pre/post test) are measured before and after their respective interventions to identify any change. Here, the research can not only pinpoint change, but also link it, or its absence, to a specific intervention. However, there may be differences among the apparently similar groups; for instance, they may all be women, but one group may have a different age, ethnicity or class mix from the other, which could also account for the different levels of change identified in each group.

To reduce the risk of bias, the best form of intervention study is seen as the Randomized Control Trial (RCT), which aims to even out the chance that different groups will be roughly similar, with the result that any changes identified in the group are more likely to be the result of the intervention than of chance. RCTs are regarded by EBSW as having the edge over other forms of intervention studies (Macdonald 2001, Sheldon and Macdonald 2008). They are, for instance, the basis of assessing and evaluating the effectiveness of new medical treatments. In their absence, quasi-experimental studies are helpful guides; and failing these, pre/post studies provide some guidance.

Box 2.3   Systematic Reviews

Many EBSW writers now identify Systematic Reviews as the new 'gold standard' of evidence about the effectiveness of interventions (e.g. Newman et al. 2005, Sheldon and Macdonald 2008).

The Campbell Collaboration, which promotes the use of systematic reviews in social welfare, criminal justice, and education, describes systematic reviews as follows:

'The purpose of a systematic review is to sum up the best available research on a specific question. This is done by synthesizing the results of several studies.

A systematic review uses transparent procedures to find, evaluate and synthesize the results of relevant research. Procedures are explicitly defined in advance, in order to ensure that the exercise is transparent and can be replicated. This practice is also designed to minimize bias.

Studies included in a review are screened for quality, so that the findings of a large number of studies can be combined. Peer review is a key part of the process; qualified independent researchers control the author's methods and results.' http://camp.ostfold.net/what_is_a_systematic_review/index.shtml

However, systematic reviews should be treated carefully. They may not include the most up-to-date research, and any recommendations and conclusions that they draw should be recognized as the reviewer's opinion, not fact (Macdonald 2003). The key to evaluating a systematic review is its protocol, which lets you know how the review was conducted and the process by which it was originally constructed, and by which it is kept up to date.

Campbell Collaboration (C2) Social Welfare Co-ordinating Group website provides further information about systematic reviews (including examples) are: http://www.campbellcollaboration.org/SWCG/index.asp

The concerns underpinning the hierarchy of evidence posited by EBSW are the reduction of bias in specifying change and identifying any intervention associated with that change.

In this outline of EBSW, we have sought to identify how EBSW has translated to social work the evidence-based approach developed in medicine. The basic structure of EBM – the idea that practice should be informed by a critical dialogue of external evidence, professional judgement and theory – has something to contribute to current debates about knowledge and practice in social work. However, EBSW has tended to use an evidence-based approach to criticize professional judgement and the use of theory, rather than seeing them as key sources of evidence. In translating EBM from medicine to social work, it is important to recognize not only what it has to offer, but also its possible limitations. From the preceding account, it is clear that EBSW has adopted the same idea of good-quality research evidence as that used in medicine. But social work is not medicine. The nature of social workers' interventions is different from, say, the drug treatments employed by doctors. In the remainder of this chapter we want to consider: the appropriateness for social work of the hierarchy of evidence to which EBSW subscribes; and the broader implications of EBSW for the nature and role of social work.

Science, evidence and practice

Here we want to look at two key concerns about EBSW's commitment to scientific evidence as the best evidence to guide social work practice. The first relates to its knowledge claims; and the second involves practical problems in its implementation.

The first area of concern relates to the claims that EBSW makes about there being a hierarchy of knowledge, with some forms of research providing more precision and certainty about social interventions than others. Knowledge about 'what works' is clearly relevant in social work and EBSW often refers to the success of Randomized Control Trials (RCTs) in determining how well drugs work, and implies that they will have similar success in the evaluation of social interventions. However, can the method of medical intervention be applied to social work? Interventions are very different things. They are based on different frameworks of knowledge and methods and contexts of administering help. Medicine as a profession, for instance, is based on research knowledge from the basic natural sciences, and primarily focuses on the body as a bio-chemical organism. Employing experimental methods from the natural sciences in social enquiry is unlikely to yield certainty to the same degree possible in the medical sciences. Ziman (1978), for instance, points out that social enquiry is concerned with the complex and dynamic material and that in making enquiries about human behaviour: '...we can seldom make a sharply confirmable (or disconfirmable) prediction...statistical argument never actually confirms a hypothesis; it can only tell us, more or less loosely, whether the data are consistent with our theoretical assumptions...Statistical inferences from data with large and uncontrollable variances are often "interesting" but seldom convincing' (ibid.: 169–70). While scientific methods make a valuable contribution to the study of social phenomena, we should not assume, as EBSW does, that they have the same predictive power or authority as they have on home ground in the biomedical sciences.

Another dimension of EBSW's claim for the authority of scientific research, and the idea of a hierarchy of research evidence, is that, unlike many other forms of social enquiry, it can reduce the influence of subjectivity, equating subjectivity with bias. Its concerns for rigour are important; but it is problematic to assume that it is unique in these concerns. Casting good-quality social enquiry in terms of the elimination of subjectivity assumes that subjective understanding and empathetic insight are unnecessary in understanding fellow humans; and that the elimination of subjectivity from the social sciences is possible and desirable. Both these assumptions are dubious. Ziman, for instance, points out that: 'In every historical, sociological, anthropological, or psychological situation there are, of course, many elements and factors capable of rigorous logical analysis, but factors of emotion and human value cannot be brought into public discussion without an appeal to the empathetic authority of the common humanity of actors and observer' (ibid.: 178).This is not a claim that we can simply step into one another's shoes; but, he argues, it is possible to draw analogies with our own experiences that help us to understand others and to talk sensibly about these things with one another. Social knowledge is fuzzier than the sharp-edged categories of natural sciences, but that does not make it less rigorous or insightful. Furthermore, in the analysis of social situations, and given the impact one can have on them, the scientific stance is a choice. It is a choice of how to see the world: seeing the facts starts with choosing which facts to see. Sheldon, for instance, acknowledges that 'Human subjects differ greatly in their experiences, their socio-economic circumstance, their interest in what is being investigated etc. The only way to iron out these differences is by random selection and stratification.'

(Sheldon 2001: 804). However, choosing to 'iron out' differences is not a matter of fact; it reflects one's own preferences and view of the world (Midgley 2001).

A wider range of research methods can provide important and relevant guidance to professionals about working with service users. An example of the role of, say, a qualitative research approach is helpful here. According to the hierarchy of knowledge proposed by EBSW, quantitative research is the best way to establish the relationship between what is done and its outcome. However, Merton, in his account of the development of focus groups as a research method, explains that these were originally developed because of the limitations of quantitative research in specifying the impact of public information films (and intervention) on their audience (population); 'The resulting qualitative material did much to help shape the interpretation of the quantitative data' (Merton 1987: 555). Evidence about 'what works' (and explanations of why it might work) in social work is likely to be more democratic and less hierarchical than EBSW would have us believe.

Another concern about EBSW's approach to evidence is that it is over-ambitious. The key problem here is the paucity of the forms of evidence that, EBSW argues, social workers should use. Scientific evidence about what works, particularly RCTs and systematic reviews, is thin on the ground in social work, particularly outside the USA (Sheldon and Macdonald 2008). In fact, EBSW acknowledges that the high costs of research, technical problems in evaluating social interventions and complex ethical issues make producing this sort of evidence a challenge. But it doesn't see these problems as insurmountable. Rather, EBSW points to a bright new dawn of good-quality evidence, but one that is always just over the horizon (Macdonald 1994, 2001, 2002; Sheldon and Macdonald 2008).

In the meantime, EBSW has two strategies for dealing with the problem of the paucity of what it sees as good evidence for practice. One is to acknowledge, reluctantly, that social work has to be informed by other forms of evidence – from the lower levels of the hierarchy of evidence – while warning that this evidence should be used in the knowledge that it is lower grade and limited (Macdonald 2002). The other strategy is to search for and take 'good-quality' evidence from other contexts – professionally and geographically (Gibbs and Gambrill 2002; Macdonald 2001, 2003). Social work journals might be the natural starting point for seeking research evidence, but they are only one possible source. The EBSW practitioner needs to overcome disciplinary and national bias and look for relevant material, wherever it can be found. The *British Journal of Psychiatry*, for instance, is as likely to yield good-quality evidence as the *British Journal of Social Work*, and studies from the US have as much to tell us about what does or doesn't work as evidence from the UK.

The clear problem here is that evidence from these different contexts often entails knowledge and assumptions specific to these disciplines and cultures. Proponents of EBSW accept that transferability of research from one context to another can give rise to difficulties. They concede that transferability can be a fundamental problem in relation to research that evaluates the impact of social policy interventions, which it accepts are context sensitive. However, they argue that problems of transferability are unlikely to arise:

> where inter- or intra-personal interventions are based on empirically validated theories of human behaviour, such as social learning theory. The principles of social learning theory…are universal in their application…The interpretation of research findings and their application needs to be culture-, gender- and class-specific, but their validity is not intrinsically threatened by changes of government or geographical boundaries. Similar arguments are tenable with regard to therapeutic interventions. (Macdonald 2001: 23)

The argument seems to be that evidence from one culture can be applied in any other, because science has established that, underneath minor local differences, there is a universally true human core, as described by social learning theory. However the empirical validation of a theory does not make it true; certainly not universal (Ziman 1991: Sheldon 2001). The implication would be that – knowing what is universally true – we merely need to read the right text book. Yet the universality of social learning theory is far from established. Behaviourism, for instance – a key element of social learning theory – is not universally accepted. Midgley, for instance, points out that psychology has had to abandon the principles of behaviourism as implausible: 'The attempt to study behaviour without considering the motives behind it could not work because it is not really possible to observe and describe behaviour at all (apart from the very simplest actions) without grasping the motives that it expresses' (Midgley 2001:93).

EBSW: evidence in whose interest?

The other set of questions about EBSW relates to its idea of the role of social work and its ethical and political commitments, particularly its relationship with managerialism. Webb has argued that in '... evidence-based practice effectiveness sits comfortably alongside the new managerialism in social work...this narrow view of the world endorses the idea that practice should be first and foremost objectively accountable to administrative functions and controls' (Webb 2001: 74).

Managerialism entails the combination of two phenomena: the increasing organizational control and regulation of professional practice within social services; and the colonization of professional practice by financial priorities and concerns such as cost control and rationing at the expense of traditional values that focus on the needs of service users (Evans 2009). EBSW accepts management control of certain aspects of professional practice. Advocates of EBSW, such as Macdonald, have argued that social workers should accept management direction to relieve them of concerns for broad and vague commitments in professional codes. In this bargain with management, social workers retain an expertise-based freedom to do their job, in return for accepting organizational objectives:

> The moral constraints that social workers require are not admonitions to 'care' but the constraints afforded by, for instance, structured supervision, goal setting and case closure. If corners are to be cut and possibilities for action time limited (that is, any emergency attended to will mean disattending to other situations) it becomes the responsibility of organizations to face these pressures squarely and 'come clean' about the boundaries of acceptable deferment and non-performance ...the organizations in which they [social workers] work could, and should, facilitate the optimum execution of that remit and relieve some of the conflicting pressure that exact such a heavy toll on workers. (Macdonald 1990: 542)

Guidelines and directives are also accepted as appropriate to structure professional practice, but as these should be based on research evidence they support rather than undermine professional discretion (Macdonald 1994: 426).

It is possible to distinguish two forms of workers' freedom from organizational control: ideological freedom (control over the goal of work) and technical freedom (control over means and methods in doing the job) (Deber 1983). Using this distinction, EBSW's stance could be seen as an astute professional strategy to retain technical freedom by relinquishing ideological freedom. This has been an established strategy in traditional social work (Harris 1998). But the question of EBSW's relationship to managerialism is more complex. The key issue here is: on what basis has EBSW struck its bargain on professional freedom? To what extent does the balance of freedom and constraint enhance or inhibit social work's professional commitments to service users?

Hudson and Roberts give the basic reasons for choosing EBSW as ethical; that is: '...to get the best available help [for service-users, and]...secondary to this motivation is the professional and managerial issue: accountability to taxpayers and employers is also an ethical consideration' (Hudson and Roberts 1998: 154). Furthermore, advocates of EBSW are interested in the efficiency and effectiveness of interventions. For Newman et al., in fact: '...efficient use of public money is another reason to ensure that care is provided based on evidence of what is thought to work best for service users. Efficiency is an essential corollary of effectiveness' (Newman et al. 2005:8).

The interests of taxpayers and service users often do not coincide – a lesson that has been hammered home in the welfare services over the past decades (Timmins 1995). Furthermore, efficiency is not a direct and natural consequence of effectiveness; they are, in fact, very different notions. Effectiveness is concerned with what works, what is capable of producing the desired result. In contrast, the concern of efficiency is achieving a goal by expending the least effort/cost. The most efficient service may not be the most effective: practitioners may want the most effective service for users, but tax payers may not be willing to pay for it. These conflicts are staple themes in news coverage of public services, with frequent stories about service users denied the help they need because of the cost and drugs, prescribed as the most effective treatment, being denied because they were not cost effective.

Webb criticizes EBSW for its commitment to effectiveness; but surely the issue is that EBSW's commitment to efficiency, rather than to effectiveness, is professionally controversial. Few, apart from Webb, would criticize social work for seeking to make itself more useful to the people it serves (Smith 2004). In this sense, EBSW's concern for effectiveness is a long-standing and shared concern of professional social work – although there are different ways of approaching the idea of effectiveness. The problem of EBSW is that it has surreptitiously eroded this professional commitment in social work by eliding it with managerial concerns for efficiency, for cost and tax-payer value. It is in this respect that EBSW identifies itself with managerialism.

There are many elements of EBSW that require fuller explanation. How, for instance, does it balance effectiveness and efficiency in practice? How would an EBSW practitioner respond when faced with conflicts between the interests of the service-user and tax-payers' interests? How do its choices about priorities and rights sit with its apparently apolitical 'unbiased' self-image? Macdonald claims that EBSW eschews politics by accepting the priorities set by managers; is this plausible?

Conclusion

Evidence-based practice in medicine developed as a response to the need to evaluate an increasingly complex body of research and to incorporate this research into clinical practice. The proponents of evidence-based social work are surely right in identifying the idea of EBM as relevant to debates about the role of external evidence in improving social work interventions. However, EBSW's approach to practice and evidence raises significant questions about its translation of EBM into a social work context. EBM's potential contribution to the social work debate about the relationship of evidence and practice lies in its recognition of the role of good-quality external evidence alongside professional judgement and theory. It portrays these elements in terms of critical dialogue between different sources of evidence-informing practice decision-making. In contrast, EBSW puts forward a more limited idea of a monologue of research evidence, critical of practice intuition and theory. Even though there is an increasing recognition within EBSW of the role of professional judgement, this does not seem to match Sackett et al.'s observation that good practice involves:

> both individual clinical expertise and the best available external evidence, neither alone is good enough. Without clinical expertise, practice risks becoming tyrannized by evidence, for even excellent external evidence may be inapplicable to or inappropriate for an individual patient. Without current best evidence, practice risks becoming rapidly out of date, to the detriment of patients. (Sackett et al. 1996: 71)

While social work can learn from medicine – as medicine can learn from social work – social work is not medicine. Accordingly, in applying the ideas of EBM to social work, we have to be aware of differences as well as similarities. EBSW's proponents' belief that good-quality evidence in social work can be assessed according to the same standards of evidence applied in the medical sciences is more open to debate than they acknowledge. The idea that there is a hierarchy of evidence that should guide social work interventions is problematic, both because social scientific evidence is unlikely to yield the level of certainty that scientific evidence can; and because effective evaluation of social work practice requires a broad and variegated body of evidence.

Social work practice exists in an ethical and political context. Questions have been raised about the relationship of EBSW to this context. Its emphasis on social work as an expert, technical activity might, in some circumstances, be an argument to defend professional status and discretion. However, its commitment to efficiency as much as effectiveness in practice points to fundamental tensions in its ethical stance that need to be addressed.

Box 2.3

The critical thinking tool you should use to evaluate Bradshaw (2003) is the Quasi-Experimental Study Tool and the Qualitative Research Tool for Kim and Fox (2006).

3

Service Users: Justice and Power?

'Principles of human rights and social justice are fundamental to social work.' (International Federation of Social Workers 2000)

Traditionally, professionals are not only understood as workers with particular expertise, but also as workers who use this expertise in the interests of the people for whom they work (Freidson 2001). This self-image of professional social work has been subject to increasing challenge from service users. On what basis is it that social workers know what is best to do? What is the basis of their expertise about the lives of service users? What do they know about the preferences and hopes of other people? In whose interests do social workers act? These questions are wide-ranging, and in this chapter we will look at them in relation to the research knowledge about service users that social workers employ in their practice.

A particular problem here is that what constitutes good-quality knowledge about service users is controversial. Research about service users in social care is not new. There is a long tradition of professional researchers investigating the lives of people to identify their needs, and the ways in which they can be helped and their lives changed (Barnes 2003). However, service users are increasingly questioning the rights of researchers to speak on their behalf, and to investigate issues without consulting the people who are being researched (ibid.: Hanley 2005). One concern is the relationship between the researcher and the researched, in terms of how the research is done. A particular criticism here is that researchers treat service users simply as research subjects – sources of information to be mined and then discarded. Another concern builds on this to question the priorities of researchers themselves, and their understanding of the consequences of their work for the people involved. Service user organizations point out that their priorities are often quite different, and that researchers fail to take these into account. These two broad areas interrelate, but for the sake of clarity we will distinguish them as: debates about how research should be conducted – that is, how the practice of research can be moved in a more participatory direction from research 'on' service users to research 'with' service users; and the control of research – who sets the research agenda, and what commitments and priorities should be reflected in the practice of research with service users.

Up to this point, we have talked about 'service users'. We need to acknowledge here the diversity of people who use social care services. In a chapter such as this, it is not possible to reflect all groups, and we will focus on two particularly influential groups in service user research: feminist researchers and disabilities researchers.

Feminist research has been influential in a wide range of areas of social care research, and has also contributed to the development of arguments by particular service user groups such as disabilities rights groups (Mercer 2002). Disability research has been particularly influential in health and social care fields, addressing issues of research and users in particular. It acknowledges the contribution of feminist research to its developing thinking, and has also itself put forward influential ideas about the recasting of the role of researcher and subject, and the framework of ideas which should structure research activity (Tew et al. 2006).

Emancipation, empowerment and justice

The relationship between research, justice and empowerment is complex. Giving power to service users is a long-standing goal of public policy in social care: 'Instead of users and carers being subordinate to the wishes of service providers, the roles will be progressively adjusted. In this way, users and carers will be enabled to exercise the same power as consumers of other services' (Social Services Inspectorate, 1991, para. 6). And it is a concern that, in the form of individual budgets, has become a central concern of government policy (Department of Health 2006). However, while the goals of empowerment of service users and justice are widely accepted within social work, they are understood in a range of different ways: they are contested concepts.

Box 3.1   Empowerment

One very concrete definition of empowerment is one which ensures that users are provided with services which workers can justify in terms of their evidence base, which have a clear rationale, and in relation to which workers can state clearly how it is anticipated that these services will achieve the desired outcomes. This kind of information maximizes user choice, and gives service users a means by which to hold workers accountable for their involvement in their lives. (Macdonald 2001: 22)

Two aspects to empowerment are regularly identified: personal and political empowerment. Personal empowerment is concerned with strengthening the individual's position, through capacity and confidence building, skills and assertiveness training, to be able to gain more power. Political empowerment is concerned with seeking to make broader change that will increase the objective power (political, cultural, social and economic) available to people. A particular appeal of the idea of empowerment is the way it can address and unite these two concerns: individual and social transformation. (Beresford in Hanley et al. 2005: 15)

In Box 3.1 we give two different definitions of empowerment. Their implications for the role which research plays in social work practice as empowerment are very different. Macdonald emphasizes the importance of informing service users as consumers of professional services, by ensuring that services are guided by research and that professionals are aware of service users' preferences. Beresford offers a more wide-ranging notion of empowerment. His idea of personal empowerment could, in some respects, overlap with Macdonald's idea, but he goes on to link personal with political empowerment, equalizing service users' access to power in society. Beresford's notion relates to a broader sense in which research supports the goal of empowerment, in that its role is to transform the place of people who use services in society in a number of ways – personally, by being involved in research, and recognizing their own ability to contribute to knowledge; and also by using research knowledge in a political struggle for equality.

These different ideas of empowerment can also suggest different ideas of justice. The emphasis on empowerment of consumers links to a market idea of justice, in which the consumers of services can exercise choices and have rights that they can demand of those who provide a professional product. The more political idea of empowerment suggests a different notion of justice related to a goal of equalizing power between people in society. In this chapter, we will focus on this second idea of justice, associated with social change; and on the idea of empowerment, which makes links between personal and political change. These ideas themselves are broad-ranging, but are captured within the overall idea of emancipatory research which: '...prioritizes the achievement of people's human and civil rights and their increased say and choices over their lives and the services they receive.' (Tew et al. 2006:15)

The problem of 'mainstream' research

Emancipatory research has developed in reaction to what it sees as the limitations of traditional and mainstream research to reflect the experiences and concerns of marginalized groups, such as service users and carers. Emancipatory research not only aims to use research to transform society, but also seeks to transform research itself, better to reflect its commitments to empowerment and justice. Its criticisms have focused on the ability of mainstream research to reflect the experiences and concerns of the people studied – how well this approach to research can reflect people's lived experience; and the purpose and use of research – who is in control of the research agenda and its impact. The focus of the criticism of social research by service users has been 'mainstream' and 'traditional' research. Hanley et al. (2005) describe this type of research as:

> research that is most often published in peer-reviewed journals. It is usually concerned with:
>
> - generating reliable, replicable knowledge
> - being 'scientific' and rigorous
> - maintaining objectivity
> - retaining 'distance' from its subject matter
> - being neutral, impartial and avoiding value-based judgements.
>
> Randomized controlled trials have been seen as the gold standard for this type of research. (ibid.: 14)

Mainstream/traditional research, then, in the view of Hanley et al., is research that aims to be objective and disinterested and that seeks to establish scientific truth.

Box 3.2   Reflective Question

Think back to the preceding chapter on evidence-based practice: do you think Hanley et al.'s characterization of mainstream/traditional research is a fair characterization of research in social work?

The criticisms of mainstream/traditional research that have emerged from service users and emancipatory researchers are that it does not provide, as it claims, an unbiased approach that simply records reality. Rather, critics argue, it presents the research process as a logical, linear process to cloak its reliance on hunches and assumptions and to protect them from challenge. Its 'hygienic' picture of research, while misleading, is useful because it makes researchers look like technical experts standing above the fray. However, contrary to this flattering self-image, critics suggest, mainstream research does not eliminate bias; it simply naturalizes the researchers' own assumptions, and takes the views of powerful groups in society for granted. Portraying social enquiry as science also allows – and requires – researchers to treat those studied as objects rather than as agents; and this gives rise to criticism of mainstream research as ethically insensitive.

Emancipatory researchers have challenged the claims to 'objective' and 'unbiased' knowledge put forward by mainstream research (Barnes 1996). Feminist researchers, for instance, have sought to unmask gendered assumptions in mainstream research, pointing to the way in which researchers have frequently naturalized stereotypes that associate men with reason and logic, and devalue emotion and subjectivity, which they have equated with femininity (Grimshaw 1986). Similarly, disability activists have challenged unfounded assumptions in studies of people with disabilities. They point, for instance, to the 'conventional wisdom' contained in a large body of welfare research, that: '...accredited impairment, whether physical, sensory or intellectual, is the primary cause of "disability" and therefore [of] the difficulties: economic, political and cultural, encountered by people labelled "disabled"' (Barnes 2003: 4). But why, these critics ask, should we assume that the 'disabled' individual should be seen as the problem, the focus of enquiry? What about the impact of society on its 'disabled' members? Oliver illustrates this problem by contrasting different approaches to constructing questions for a survey of disability need. He takes a question from an official government survey that asks 'Can you tell me what is wrong with you?' and suggests another question that could replace it: 'Can you tell me what is wrong with society?' (Oliver 1992:104). Why, he asks, does the official survey question simply reinforce commonplace assumptions about the individual nature of disability, and not ask the question which is more enquiring and critical? The assumptions of researchers, in effect, deny their subjects the right to talk about the world in their own terms.

The perceived mis-match between researchers' assumptions and people's lived experience has also led to concern about the power of the researchers. A key aspect of mainstream research, these critics argue, is the emphasis on the need for distance between researcher and research subject. The researcher aims to stand aside from the concerns and interests of the people being studied to see the picture clearly (Tew et al. 2006). However this stance fails to recognize that research subjects are, like the researcher, human beings. In denying this shared humanity, mainstream research not only dehumanizes people as 'research subjects', but also treats them unethically as means and not ends in themselves (Midley 2001). Mainstream research, it is argued, denies people's ability to play an active role in developing knowledge about their situation. It 'does' research 'to' subjects – from the point of view that it knows best – and shoehorns complex social issues into a predetermined framework. Accordingly, it fails to recognize that research participants have their own concerns about what should be researched, their own explanations of the social world that are at least as valid as those of researchers (see Box 3.3).

The observation that mainstream researchers are able to impose their views on research subjects, critics argue, raises questions about whose interests mainstream research is promoting. The conclusion of many marginalized groups is that mainstream research has not promoted their interests and that this needs to change: 'the social relations of research production...have to be fundamentally changed; researchers have to learn how to put their knowledge and skills at the disposal of their research subjects, for them to use in whatever ways they choose' (Oliver 1992: 111).

Researchers committed to emancipatory goals have sought to address the problems they identify in mainstream research by developing methods that acknowledge and value a commitment to justice and empowerment, and work with research participants as equals. Here, we want to consider two broad approaches to this challenge that can overlap. One has been a focus on developing an emancipatory method of social research; the other has been increasing the role and power of service users within the research process.

Box 3.3 The Problem of Disinterested Research?

An influential piece of research in the development of the disabilities rights movement was Miller and Gwynne's 'A Life Apart'. Miller and Gwynne were invited to do an in-depth study of a group home by its residents, to support their struggle with the home's management for more control over their lives (Barnes and Mercer 1997). However, in the words of one resident, Paul Hunt, the residents came to realize that the researchers: 'were definitely not on our side. They were not really on the side of the staff either. And they were not even much use to the management and administrators. They were in fact basically on their own side, that is the side of supposedly "detached", "balanced", "unbiased" social scientists, concerned above all with presenting themselves to the powers-that-be as indispensable in training "practitioners" to manage the problem of disabled people in institutions'. (Hunt 1981)

In a later study, Miller and Gwynne explained in *A Life Apart*:

> We were into an 'enlightenment' model of social research. Essentially this meant starting from a study of behaviour – what people were actually doing and their own descriptions of it. Human problems...do not fit into the compartments of scientific discipline; so we had to find ways of describing, understanding, and explaining behaviour that made sense both to ourselves and to the client groups, and, in addition, gave them some leverage for thinking about possible change...Our aim – not always achieved – was to illuminate what they were doing and why it seemed they were doing it, so that they themselves could make up their minds about whether and what to change. (Dartington, Miller and Gwynne 1981: 10–11)

Their approach included recognizing and acknowledging their own 'mixed and conflicting feelings' (ibid.: 13). However, here they noted that:

> Our open confession of ambivalence got us into trouble in some quarters: if we held attitudes that were so plainly outdated and wrong, how could our analysis of residential care be taken seriously?...Some of the criticisms levelled against this piece of work were valid, some less so. The fact that we described what seemed to be happening did not mean that we approved of it; but the messenger always runs the risk of being shot. (ibid.: 13 and 16)

- Do you think researchers should take sides?
- If so whose side?
- What impact does taking sides have on how fair/balanced research might be?

You can read Hunt's account of the research and his reaction to it in 'Settling Accounts with the Parasite' at: http://www.leeds.ac.uk/disabilitystudies/archiveuk/UPIAS/Disability%20Challenge1.pdf

You can find references for Miller and Gwyne's original study (Miller and Gwyne 1972) and their reflections of responses to it (Dartington et al. 1981) in the References section.

An emancipatory method of social research?

Feminist research has played a leading role in challenging the scientific myth of 'mainstream' research. It has also played an important part in developing and promoting qualitative research methods as an alternative to 'mainstream' research. Maynard explains that: '...the use of qualitative methods, which focus more on the subjective experiences and meaning of those being researched, was regarded as more appropriate to the kind of knowledge that feminists wished to make available, as well as being more in keeping with the politics of doing research as a feminist' (Maynard 1994: 11). Qualitative research, particularly the semi-structured and unstructured interview, has become the orthodox stance of much emancipatory research. In feminism, for instance, qualitative methods and data have come to be seen as the authentic feminist research (Maynard and Purvis 1994). In disability and service user research, researchers have tended to adopt qualitative methods (Mercer 2002; Tew et al. 2006).

However, there is concern among some emancipatory researchers that the recognition of the contribution of qualitative research too easily slips into a rejection of quantitative methods. Several commentators are worried that the positive contribution of quantitative research to empowerment is overlooked. Quantitative research's ability to specify the extent and impact of structural inequalities on health, life chances, access to services etc. has been an important weapon in the emancipatory armoury (Barnes 2003; Mercer 2002; Maynard and Purvis 1994; Tew et al. 2006; Truman 1999, 2000). Furthermore, Maynard argues that the problems identified by critics of quantitative research are not intrinsic to that method as such, but are the result of the influence of positivism – the view that science should be the model for social enquiry, with the researcher as an objective fact-gatherer, standing apart from the social world and affecting to study it from the outside (Blackburn 2005). The problem with quantitative research, Maynard argues, is not the quantification as an approach to understanding the social world, but those researchers: '...who regard themselves as neutral researchers producing objective and value-free "facts"'. In contrast to this she advocates quantitative research with '...more circumspect [researchers], acknowledging that providing figures involves as much of an act of social construction as any other kind of research' (Maynard 1994: 13). It has also been demonstrated that quantitative research can be conducted in partnership with service users. Truman, for instance,

---

Box 3.4   Radical Statistics

The Radical Statistics Group, usually abbreviated to Radstats, was formed in 1975...Members are 'radical' in being committed to helping build a more free, democratic and egalitarian society. Members of Radstats are concerned at the extent to which official statistics reflect governmental rather than social purposes. Our particular concerns are:

- The mystifying use of technical language to disguise social problems as technical ones
- The lack of control by the community over the aims of statistical investigations, the way these are conducted and the use of the information produced
- The power structures within which statistical and research workers are employed and which control the work and how it is used
- The fragmentation of social problems into specialist fields, obscuring connectedness

You can find out more about radical statistics at: http://www.radstats. org.uk/about.htm

---

argues that, 'Given the privileged status of quantitative data, it is imperative that the less powerful are able to shape this form of knowledge. The technical competence of researchers can enable this to happen...Involving the less powerful and marginalized in the creation of social statistics means that this is precisely what they might become: social statistics, rather than anti-social statistics' (Truman 1999: 155).

The reverse side of the coin is a naive belief in the effectiveness of qualitative research in establishing democratic research relationships. However, as we saw above, in the outline of users' reaction to Miller and Gwynne's research (Box 2.1), it was the expert distance and analytic stance of qualitative researchers conducting an in-depth study that alienated the residents of Le Court (Hunt 1981; Barnes and Mercer 1997; Mercer 2002).

User involvement in research

Researchers have sought to ensure that research is better able to reflect people's views, and recognize them as fellow human beings within a research process, rather than passive research subjects.

There is little disagreement that user involvement in research is not only a moral imperative (Fisher 2002, Tew et al. 2006), but that it is also essential to improve research knowledge. Users and carers '...can bring "added value" to all stages of the research process' (Tew et al. 2006: 23), and can '...undoubtedly improve the quality' of research such as systematic reviews (Macdonald 2003: 11).

A further aspect of this development is a concern to involve service users in broader issues, designing studies, and making decisions about their implementation and the dissemination of research findings (Barnes 2003; Fisher 2002; Hanley 2005; Oliver 1992; Tew 2006; Truman et al. 2000).

Fisher (2002), for instance, identifies three key dimensions in which user involvement enhances the quality of research knowledge and its relevance, and reflects an emancipatory stance. Firstly, users should be involved in identifying the main research problems and data, and prioritizing research activity. They should have a central role in setting the agenda. Related to this, they should also be involved in identifying and accessing relevant and significant sources of information in the research process. Secondly, recognizing that research is an increasingly important element in service development, the preferred outcomes and values of users should play an important role in service evaluations, which should move beyond just the official focus on effectiveness and efficiency to reflect concerns about good-quality service on the ground. Finally, service users should be involved in the analysis of research. Here, Fisher illustrates the point with his own experience, pointing to a situation where, in reviewing research data, a comment was made in an interview about the role of panels in making decisions about service provision. This comment did not appear important to him because it was a one-off, but his fellow (service user) researchers identified it as significant. It resonated with their experience, and captured something that was so often not voiced, because it was such a commonplace experience of having to justify demands for services.

However, the precise nature of user involvement in research has given rise to sharp debate. While there is clear agreement that service users should be involved throughout the research process, there are very different views about the nature of this involvement – is it partnership, control, or leadership? To what extent do researchers retain an independent perspective? What are the demands of commitment, loyalty and accountability on researchers?

Oliver has argued for a fundamental shift in what he calls 'the structural relations of research', a change from researcher control to service user control of research. Barnes also argues that disabilities organizations should own and control service user research (Barnes 2003:13). However, control, it is argued by some advocates of emancipatory research, has to be more than about replacing non-service-user researchers with service user researchers, and having user organizations commissioning research. This research has to be committed to the right perspective:

> In practice disabled researchers, as well as the disabled individuals who have a controlling interest in a research project, may only become the new 'experts', 'professionals' or 'elite', replacing people with abilities who have traditionally been in this relationship to those being researched. All too often, we can be deluded by contemporary language to regard a project as involving emancipatory research, while in reality the substance of the research is actually traditional and sympathetic to the individual model of disability...Is the social model of disability a tool for focusing a microscope on the inner workings of the disabling society or merely a frame holding a magnifying glass for exaggerating the social experiences of disabled people living in the disabling society? (Finkelstein 1999: 861)

The social model of disability

The social model of disability was developed within the context of the disability rights movement (Oliver 1991; Barnes and Mercer 1997), but it has become increasingly influential in the wider emancipatory research (Truman 2000; Tew et al. 2006).

The social model of disability entails a series of key contrasts (Shakespeare 2006). The first is the distinction between an individualized, biological account of disability and the social model itself. The biological account focuses on physical impairment as the key to understanding disability. The problems that people with disabilities face are the result of their physical impairments. The limitations to access to buildings etc. are explained by limited limb movement, for instance. In contrast to this perspective, the social model draws a clear distinction between impairment and disability. Impairment is biological and physical. It is the fact of spinal injury, for instance, which restricts limb movement. Disability is quite different. It relates to the social experience of people who have impairments, in terms of their limited opportunities and the disadvantages they face. The problem of access, from this perspective, is not lack of limb movement or the use of a wheelchair, but the absence of dropped kerbs, ramps and lifts. This distinction between impairment and disability is placed in a wider social context, which identifies disabled people as being oppressed by non-disabled people, and requires the analysis of disability to acknowledge this dichotomy and to identify itself either with the interests of people with disabilities or with the interests of the major part of society that oppresses them:

> Researchers should not be professing 'mythical independence' to disabled people, but joining with them in their struggle to confront and overcome this oppression. Researchers should be espousing commitment, not value freedom; engagement, not objectivity; and solidarity, not independence. There is no independent haven or middle ground when researching oppression. Academics and researchers can only be with the oppressors or with the oppressed. (Barnes 1996: 110)

The idea that the principles of the social model should necessarily structure user research is not unanimously accepted (Shakespeare 1996, 2006; Stone 1997). Shakespeare (1996), for instance, distinguishes involving and sharing power with research subjects from the idea of researching under the control of disabilities organizations. He is concerned that advocates of user-control seek to replace commitment with uncritical loyalty. Loyalty, he argues is a threat to good-quality critical research: 'I believe it is sometimes my duty to be critical, to raise questions and consider issues which may have been overlooked...an organization may become unrepresentative, or may act in ways which do not seem to be in the best interests of the disability community as a whole or sections of it. In that context, it is the right, indeed, possibly the duty of academics, to take an independent line' (Shakespeare 1996: 117).

Furthermore, the assertion that the model presents a clear, self-evident framework within which to conduct emancipatory user research is contentious (see Box 3.5). A major concern about the social model is its inflexible distinction between 'impairment' and 'disability' (Shakespeare 2006). There are two elements of concern here. The first is that by seeing 'impairment' as individual, physical and biological, the social model, as an agenda for research, brackets off questions of how impairment may itself be socially structured. The risk with this is that it plays down important questions about the impact of, for instance, poverty on ill health, working conditions on industrial diseases and the social construction of disease, which

Box 3.5   Reflective Exercise

Go to: http://www.leeds.ac.uk/disability-studies/archiveuk/UPIAS/fundamental%20principles.pdf to read an account of a meeting involving Paul Hunt and Vic Finkelstein from The Union of the Physically Impaired Against Segregation (UPIAS an organization committed to the social model of disability, and Peter Townsend, a social policy researcher.

After reading the account, make a note of your reactions to the exchange.

are clearly significant questions (Moon et al. 2000). In treating impairment as a given, the social model risks reinforcing rather than challenging the dominant role of mainstream bio-medical research.

The second dimension is that the social model's focus on disability as exclusion seems to entail the minimization of people's experiences as 'impairment and individualistic concerns' (Mercer 2002: 335). Writers such as French have challenged the oppressive potential within the social model by which: '...my experiences are compartmentalized, with someone else being the judge of which are and which are not worthy of consideration. This gives rise to feelings of estrangement and alienation' (French 1993: 19). In his review of the social model as a framework for research, Shakespeare concludes that he finds:

> the social model unhelpful in understanding the complex interplay of individual and environmental factors in the lives of disabled people...A social approach to disability is indispensable. The medicalization of disability is inappropriate and an obstacle to effective analysis and policy. But the social model is only one of the available options for theorizing disability. More sophisticated and complex approaches are needed...(Shakespeare 2006: 202–3)

Standpoint knowledge

Up to this point we have looked at substantive arguments about how user-research should be conducted, who should control it and the idea that it should entail a commitment to a particular framework of analysis. An idea that has run through these arguments – implicitly and explicitly – has been that service users are experts 'in and by their own experience'.

Is a man who hears voices best placed to know how those voices affect him? How much of a say should he have in his treatment? Or, to put it another way, how much respect should you and other professionals accord his experience?

This idea entails two claims. The first is an ethical demand that people involved in research should not be treated as means but as ends in themselves: they should be recognized as the best judges of their own interests, and the best informants about their experience. The second claim is very different: it relates to ideas about the nature of knowledge and how we know the world around us. This claim is that, through experience, service users as a community have acquired a particularly powerful and insightful understanding of the social world. From the preceding discussion in this chapter it is clear that the ethical demand for respect for research subjects and their right to be involved as partners in research is widely accepted and established. However, the idea that user knowledge is a more insightful form of knowledge is contentious. In the final section we will examine this proposition.

We will consider the claims about the authoritative and special status of user expertise through the influential idea of 'standpoint knowledge'. This idea was developed within feminism (Harding 2004) but its influence has extended far wider within the emancipatory movement's understanding of knowledge (Cohen-Mitchell 2000; Harding 2004; Humphries 2000; Oliver 1991; Tew et al. 2006). The idea of standpoint knowledge has been employed to make the link between the particular experience of service users and emancipatory knowledge, as in mental health, where: '...mental health service users...through their process of recovery, arrive at insights and meanings in relation to their mental health distress, and also firsthand knowledge of what may have been empowering and what may have been oppressive within their experience of psychiatric services' (Tew et al. 2006: 8–9). At the core of standpoint knowledge is the idea that day-to-day experience gives people a clear view of society, how it works and in whose interest it operates. Powerful groups manage society in a way that is in their interests, to the disadvantage of the powerless. For instance, people who use wheelchairs are in a minority; most people walk. It is no more 'natural' for buildings to have stairs than to have ramps, but they tend to have stairs because this suits most people. People who use wheelchairs then have to cope with a world that is organized against their interests. As a result of their day-to-day experience, they come to see that, beneath the rhetoric of equality, society is systematically organized to put them at a disadvantage. They can use this insight to question and challenge what society takes for granted, pointing out the contradiction between talk of equality and their lived experience of inequality. It is through ordinary everyday experience of the contradictions between rhetoric and reality that marginalized groups are better able to identify the underlying structure of power that is taken for granted and goes unrecognized and unchallenged in the mainstream.

However, while standpoint knowledge entails a shared commitment to learning from the lived experience of oppressed and marginalized groups, within this approach there is a range of viewpoints about: the relationship between people's experiences and their knowledge of social oppression; and whether there is only one or several standpoints.

The first set of debates relates to the question: does standpoint knowledge arise from experience as such, or from experience that has been subjected to theoretical critique?

One approach sees 'standpoint' as accessing ways of understanding and experiencing the world which are often excluded by the mainstream. Here, experience encapsulates tacit knowledge; and researchers seek to access this unspoken knowledge, which, in turn, points up deficiencies in current understanding and extends and augments knowledge better to reflect a broad understanding of social reality. This is based on the recognition that:

> There are and must be different experiences of the world and different bases of experience. We must not do away with them by taking advantage of our privileged speaking to construct a sociological version which we then impose upon them as their reality...their reality, their varieties of experience must be an unconditional datum. (Smith 2004a: 30)

Here, then, standpoint knowledge entails the experience of marginalized groups in their own terms '...taken seriously, undistilled, untranslated' (Smith 2004b: 267); and the researcher's role is to listen to people speaking for themselves, telling their own story. This commitment is echoed in French's concerns about an imposition of other people's theories on her experience, which denies the authority of her viewpoints.

However, another view is that standpoint knowledge provides an alternative picture of the world, which is different from raw experience and superior to mainstream knowledge (Hartsock 2004 a, b).

Here, standpoint knowledge is the result of a process of critical reflection and theorizing on experience better to account for the way in which society operates. Existing knowledge is inextricably tied in to the existing social order, and standpoint knowledge can point this out and offer an alternative to it that unmasks the operation of society and provides powerful ideas with which to challenge the assumed, 'natural' order of things. This approach promotes the theories developed as a result of experience over experience itself. The social model of disability is an example of this approach. It was developed by disabled people from their experience of society, and is, in the view of many of its adherents, a complete and correct view which supercedes particular experiences. Some proponents of this view of standpoint have sought to reconcile it with diversity (Tew et al. 2006), but the tension in this approach is apparent in the observation that: 'There is a need to respect people's own understandings even when they seem to some to be an example of "internalized oppression"' (ibid.: 9).

This approach to standpoint is based on a belief that knowledge arises through a struggle with experience (Tew et al. 2006). It draws on the ideas – via Marxism – of Hegel (Zaleswski 2003). However, for Hegel, this process of developing knowledge was a continual engagement with experience, challenging the currently dominant viewpoint, and thereby causing it to be reviewed and revised (Hegel 1977; Singer 1983). It is therefore problematic to consider current knowledge – even standpoint knowledge – as conclusive.

Another important question raised by the idea of standpoint knowledge is: does the particular experience of one community mean that its standpoint provides uniquely valuable insight? In part, any answer to this question involves a challenge to the idea of the conflict of distinct and opposite groups. And yet, standpoint knowledge is often presented by its advocates as based on a distinct group, which is different from and in opposition to a dominant group in society. This view of society in terms of a dramatic distinction between oppressed and oppressor, each with an homogenous identity, has been criticized for its essentialism: the idea that members of one group are in essence the same as each other and in essence different from members of the other group. The problem here is that society and its members are multi-faceted, and far more complex than is suggested by this 'either/or' thinking. Society is not just made up of one group or another, but of many groups; and people are not just members of one group or another, but of several, often overlapping and dynamic groupings.

These and other arguments have contributed to a perspective within standpoint theory that is critical of the idea that it reveals new and superior truths. Critics fear that this approach merely replaces one dominant view with another. They prefer to see the standpoint of marginalized people as a position of critical insight, challenging and questioning generally accepted views of the world. These critics do not seek to establish a new truth, but to keep open a critical challenge, creating spaces for different viewpoints which entails: '...a continuing struggle to throw off the regulating "regimes of truth", whatever form they take – an acceptance of the permanent partiality of the point of view of those of us seeking to construct emancipatory research.' (Humphries 2000: 187). They do not seek to replace one group's perspective with another, but rather recognize the relative and contingent nature of knowledge, and the problematic nature of any claims to authoritative knowledge. The task and contribution of the standpoint perspective is in debunking claims to objective knowledge made by powerful groups, and in creating spaces in which oppressed voices can be heard. Here, the contribution of research is its critical energy – a scepticism about claims to knowledge, and a continual recognition of marginalized, different and unfashionable perspectives that snap at the heels of assumptions and unquestioning ways of thinking.

Conclusion

Emancipatory research, and the experience of users of research, raise searching questions about what constitutes valid knowledge with regard to service users' experiences and insights. We have considered how research is conducted with service users, who is in control of the research process, and whose framework of ideas and concerns should structure the work of researchers. A recurring theme in this discussion has been the issue of commitment to service users' interests. Becker has highlighted the central role of this theme in any approach to research, posing the question: 'Whose side are we on?' However, he points out, while any researcher is guided by commitment, that commitment needs to be balanced with intellectual as well as methodological rigour:

> We can, for a start, try to avoid sentimentality. We are sentimental when we refuse, for whatever reason, to investigate some matter that should properly be regarded as problematic. We are sentimental, especially, when our reason is that we would prefer not to know what is

going on, if to know would be to violate some sympathy whose existence we may not even be aware of. Whatever side we are on, we must use our techniques impartially enough that a belief to which we are especially sympathetic could be proven untrue. (Becker 1967: 246)

Another theme that has underscored this discussion is the complex nature of research that seeks to engage with the dynamism and diversity of service users' life experiences and perspectives. A challenge here is to engage with this complexity rather than forcing evidence into a pre-existing theoretical model. Humphries et al. (2000) have outlined a tentative framework for anti-exclusionary research, which suggests important themes to consider when employing user research committed to social justice and empowerment:

- Are the researchers clear about how their experiences, theoretical backgrounds and power in the situation structure the research?
- Within the particular social and political context of the research, how far are research participants recognized as co-investigators?
- How far does the account of the research acknowledge the tentative and problematic dimensions of the 'truth' it presents?
- What are the wider questions – such as justice and equality – which inform the research?

In short, employing emancipatory and user research entails a critical alertness that is guided by a commitment to justice and equality and seeks to resist being cajoled by sentimentality and power.

4

Research Knowledge

It is in the area of knowledge derived from research sources that a concern with how much credence we should attribute to a knowledge claim is most developed. Within social research, issues of quality and validity are central to mainstream methodological disputes and have been influential in debates regarding if and how it may be possible to establish the status of knowledge and differentiate between competing truth claims. In this chapter we contextualize debates about the nature of knowledge and evidence in social work within wider debates in the social sciences. In order to be able to assess the strengths and limitations of particular knowledge claims, practitioners need to understand how knowledge is produced in social research. This entails familiarity with different research methods and designs, their strengths and limitations, and the relationship between the choices entailed in undertaking social research and the paradigmatic affiliations of the researcher. We will look at approaches to research which are associated with particular paradigmatic positions, and assess their strengths and weaknesses. We will begin, however, by exploring the purposes of research and how these might relate to social work via discussion of the distinctiveness of social work research.

Research purposes

Traditionally, research has aimed to generate answers to questions in the form of knowledge 'claims' which adhere to certain conventions which distinguish these from mere assertions based on opinion or belief, thus assigning them the status of knowledge. Research seeks to remedy gaps in what is known, because what is known is in some way inadequate for our purposes. According to D'Cruz and Jones, research represents 'a peculiar manifestation of a rather fundamental form of enquiry – generating information to throw light on pressing questions' (2004: 15), while Fook and Gardner refer to 'all the different ways in which we create knowledge' (2007: 28). In social work, we might undertake research because we are unsure how to proceed in relation to a problem that needs to be resolved and for which existing attempts to generate solutions have not been wholly successful. We may be keen to improve practice – the accuracy of decision-making, for example. Or we may need to better understand the mechanisms via which a particular way of doing things achieves its aims, so as to establish if and how well an intervention is working.

There are, then, various ways in which practice might gain from research. It may help illuminate both the processes and effects of practice, thus contributing to the development of disciplinary knowledge. Research which queries the actual effects of practice may help to ensure that social work does not lose sight of its core purposes. Also, there are overlaps in the process and methods of research which parallel in some ways the social work 'process' and so there is scope for some potential benefit in exploring these similarities. Rather than being seen as separate and different, social work research can therefore be seen as another method via which social work objectives might be achieved. There is a relationship between research and how we know how to respond in or to particular situations or circumstances. Research produces knowledge which is relevant to the questions that practitioners need to address and where existing knowledge is not appropriate or sufficient. There are also reciprocal links between social work theory and research, in that research knowledge is often generated consciously in order to address practice concerns, with the findings of research leading – deductively – to theoretical adaptation or development. Equally, practice informs research, as it is through the application of existing theoretical knowledge that existing knowledge claims – hypotheses, if you like – are tested.

The utility of research stems from its potential to enhance the veracity and accuracy of knowledge claims, particularly over and above the status of claims based on individual intuition or experience. By specifying particular criteria which are deemed to contribute to rigour in the production and analysis of data, and by enabling information relating to one particular case to be combined with similar related instances, the overall quality and strength of knowledge – in terms of trustworthiness and wider applicability – may be enhanced.

Although the most obvious direct potential of research knowledge, then, relates to its capacity to inform the process and practice of assessment and intervention, there is much more to the distinctiveness of social work research that needs to be explored. Before doing so, however, it is necessary to look at general social research in more depth, especially with regard to how the quality of knowledge might be assessed.

Assessing research quality

Quality in social research relates principally to the issue of trustworthiness and the criteria which are used to assess this. Certain criteria associated with positivism have come to assume privileged status here, and it is around these that discussions about how best to assess quality and trustworthiness have developed. Key concepts include reliability, which refers to the replicability of a piece of research, that is whether its findings can be checked. Also significant is the idea of validity, particularly external validity or generalizability, which refers to the extent to which findings from one particular research study might be generalized beyond the bounds of the original study. There is also an expectation that research should be objective, with the subjective beliefs of the researchers themselves controlled for to minimize the effect of bias in potentially 'skewing' research findings. 'Values' should be separated from 'knowledge', in the interests of dispassionate enquiry and therefore objective truth.

Each of these criteria – reliability, generalizability and objectivity – is, in some respect, problematic for social science. It is very difficult to replicate the exact circumstances in which a piece of social research was undertaken as human respondents are often inconsistent. It is also not always possible to construct representative samples which allow for straightforward generalization. But it is the issue of bias which is most significant, as many social researchers, particularly those who are critical or interpretivist, believe that subjectivity should not be regarded as problematic but as inherent and productive. We all have our biases and prejudices, the reasoning goes, which reflect our values, and it is not actually possible to somehow prevent these from informing research practice. To seek to detach these is to argue that research should not seek to achieve social objectives. Instead, the suggestion is that the role played by our affiliations should be explicitly and transparently acknowledged, thus enabling those who consult research to understand where that researcher is 'coming from'.

Because of such controversies, many have argued that 'naturalist' criteria are inappropriate for assessing the quality of research which has been conducted outside the positivist paradigm. Alternative criteria which are more suited to the assumptions of alternative frameworks have been developed. Perhaps the most influential is that developed by Guba and Lincoln (1982), who suggest that whatever the underpinning paradigmatic assumptions, all research shares a number of common concerns regarding truth, wider applicability, consistency and neutrality. However, the criteria which are used to assess knowledge claims will vary according to the paradigm in which they were conducted, and this is right and proper. Underlying ontological and epistemological assumptions differ. This may make comparison between competing findings arising from differing paradigms problematic, but enables the quality of knowledge claims in a particular paradigm to be differentiated more precisely. Guba and Lincoln developed the notion of 'trustworthiness', which is assessed according to criteria of dependability, credibility, transferability and confirmability. Here, there is no expectation that reliability can be assessed by repetition of measurement, given contextual variations. The notion of credibility is less rigid than internal validity, and can be demonstrated by reference to research subjects. Although non positivist researchers are less likely to be concerned with generalizing their results, there may be situations in which this is appropriate. Transferability specifies which characteristics need to be shared on a more flexible basis than has traditionally been the case. Here, similarity of context is key. Finally, given that interpretivists deny the possibility, and indeed, desirability of objectivity, the notion of confirmability replaces a concern with demonstrating neutrality. Reflexivity is key, with researchers explicitly acknowledging the roles that their own subjective values and beliefs play in the research process.

The distinctiveness of social work research

The distinctiveness of social work research is usually seen as in some way being related to the core 'mission' of social work, which is generally seen as emancipatory, concerned with equality and justice. Social work research is undertaken within the discipline of social work which is sympathetic to, or closely aligned with, this standpoint.

Many key figures put ethical and political commitments at the heart of what social work research is. There is an evident tension here, however, because established traditions within more general research claim objectivity and neutrality as defining characteristics of research knowledge.

Everitt et al. (1992) link social work research explicitly with anti-oppressive practice. Here, the function of social work research as part of an emancipatory endeavour is to expose structures and mechanisms that generate and maintain inequality. Dominelli (2005) specifies similar defining characteristics including a transformative orientation, egalitarian relationships between researchers and researched, accountability to service users through participatory methods and holistic engagement with research respondents. McLaughlin (2007) adds a concern with changing practice for the better and a dual focus on both the needs and lives of service users, but also the role which powerful elites play in the establishment and maintenance of social divisions. These ethically driven concerns are distinct to social work and thus promote research findings which are attuned to the nature and organization of social work practice, which are value driven.

What might research undertaken according to such values entail, and how is this different from what other, non social work researchers might do? Firstly, the objectification of service users as research respondents is to be avoided. Next, the actual process of undertaking research should be one in which the status of researcher as expert is replaced by emphasis on research as joint 'meaning making'. Additionally, the views and experiences of service users are validated as useful forms of knowledge in their own right. There is clearly an implication here that researchers who do not subscribe to the value base of social work may well exploit research respondents, or downplay the significance of 'lived experience' in favour of findings produced via 'expert' analysis. These points are routinely made as part of the critique of positivist research. The 'paradigm wars' are regarded by Humphries as 'a metaphor for the powerful and the powerless' (2008: 15), with positivism on the side of the powerful and alternative approaches challenging established orthodoxy. Positivism is seen as naive in its alleged commitment to research which is neutral or free from pre-existing beliefs or bias. The interpretive critique suggests that it is not possible to generate causal laws which can be generalized from one situation, given that as individuals we interpret reality in different ways. Even if it were, partisan research has potential to bring about social changes. Research, then, is inherently political, reflecting divisions within society. Positivism's stated commitment to objectivity, or value-free endeavour, is thus impossible in practice. Instead, we all bring our beliefs and assumptions to the research arena, and they have effect.

It is on this basis that social work research as an ethical and political activity concerned with social justice is advocated. This entails the explicit intertwining of social work values, investigative enquiry and the principled commitments of researchers. Notions of neutrality or impartiality are abandoned in favour of partisanship. Rather than regarding the findings of such research as potentially invalid, partisan research is seen as more honest and transparent than that which pretends to be unbiased and seeks to disguise the role that researcher subjectivity plays in the knowledge production process. The assumption is that the values and commitments underpinning the practice of researchers will mirror those which underpin the profession more broadly, in line with a commitment to social justice. There is also a commitment to rectifying power imbalances by ensuring that those who are 'on the margins' are 'heard' and that researchers do not revert to traditional 'expert/respondent' roles. A critically self-aware reflexive stance is therefore required.

Here, then, subscription to a particular epistemological worldview comes to be seen as indicative of the potential for oppressive practice. This is some leap. However, it reflects a particular view of what social work research is, with emphasis on the pursuit of social justice rather than the 'mere' creation of objective knowledge. This position is far removed from the 'norms' within established traditions of social research, social science, or science. The dividing line between research and activism arguably becomes blurred. This is compounded when we consider which 'version' of social work we are considering. Strong advocates of emancipatory social work research risk marginalizing those who are less convinced or committed to this vision. Arguably, then, social work research is as contested as social work itself.

Research mindedness in social work

Notwithstanding the divisions within social work research, the potential that research might play in practice has recently been brought to the fore via the notion of 'research mindedness'. Variously, this entails: a belief that for practitioners to maximize their potential they need to demonstrate that research evidence underpins decision-making and action (Sheldon and Macdonald 2009); a commitment to ensuring research findings inform practice (Corby 2006); an expectation that practitioners assess the effectiveness of their work (Shaw 1996); the application of specific skills to assess the relative merits of competing knowledge claims (Sheppard 2004); or an opportunity to better understand the nature of social problems and why they occur and their meaning for those involved (Humphries 2008). This latter 'version' requires 'a commitment – even a passion – on the part of practitioners and researchers...where they explore perspectives on the social issues that they care deeply about' (ibid.: 3).

Another distinctive 'take' on this issue was developed by Everitt et al. (1992). They sought to highlight the potential that an understanding of the strengths and weaknesses of different approaches to research might bring to social work. Their starting point is a commitment to a value-driven agenda in which the notion of critical, reflexive practice is to the fore. There is emphasis on participatory approaches as representing the basis for a methodology for the research minded practitioner, while social control agendas are sidelined. The role of research is seen as key in transcending the limitations of 'routine' practice, bringing to attention the role that social divisions and power relations play within society, and their significance in perpetuating oppressive systems.

This approach is critical of the dominance that the positivist worldview has held, particularly in social work. Its inherent objectivism and naturalism are deemed inappropriate to the complex, subjective nature of the social world. Objective forms of knowledge serve 'to objectify and control others' (1992: 18). The methodological and philosophical 'fit' between interpretivism and critical theory and the aims and values of social work is seen as more congruent.

Research-minded practitioners will therefore treat their work as though research and practice are not separate, mapping research techniques across the social work process. As such, they will be better able to articulate the philosophical assumptions and theoretical perspectives which underpin their actions, use these to make sense of situations, people and behaviour, and further develop theory in practice. Simply transferring research practice into social work settings, however, is potentially problematic, not least because social work entails situations in which there are competing perspectives and inadequate information but in which decisions must nevertheless be made and acted upon. The suggestion is that often such situations can be resolved via recourse to values. The implication here is that we choose the version of the truth on which we will act according to which of the options most closely corresponds with our established beliefs –

our 'standpoint'. The inherent bias in this position is justified on the basis that it is the 'correct' bias – one which is sympathetic to the needs of the 'underdogs' in society, whose 'voices' are rarely heard, and thus with the objectives of (a particular version) of social work.

Though research mindedness does not, then, resolve issues of neutrality and bias, there is clear merit in the notion of the research-minded practitioner as one who is familiar with the ways in which differing paradigms reflect different assumptions about the nature of reality and how we understand it and how these assumptions relate to positions within political and ethical debates.

Exercise

Identify three key differences between social research and social work research.

Paradigm, research design and method

Thus far we have discussed research philosophy conceptually. However, research is a practical enterprise, which means that we need to pay attention to the associations between underpinning philosophies and particular aspects of research design and method. Here, then, we discuss the strengths and limitations of designs and methods associated with particular paradigmatic positions.

The notion of incommensurability posits irreconcilable differences between alternative paradigms. It has also been suggested that there are affiliations between paradigms and particular research methodologies, on the basis that each represents certain assumptions about social reality and social problems which influence the choice of research questions, design, method and analysis. Paradigmatic affiliations therefore represent choices which reflect an individual's beliefs, values and convictions regarding the nature of the world in which we live and how we should know it. There are alternative views, however, whereby it is not philosophical position which informs research method, but practical considerations. McLaughlin argues that 'What...should drive a choice of method is not a philosophical standpoint position but a question as to what is the most appropriate tool for the task in hand' (2007: 42).

This debate also plays out in terms of the quantitative/qualitative distinction, with a suggestion that positivists tend to favour quantitative methods and interpretivists qualitative approaches. Quantitative approaches tend to emphasize the importance of objectivity, with associated efforts to 'control' for the effects of researcher bias, while in qualitative research there is an embedded commitment to acknowledging the value of subjectivity. Again then, we are on contested ground.

Qualitative research represents a diverse family of approaches with distinctive characteristics (Shaw and Gould 2001). It tends to involve 'descriptive depth', inductive knowledge generation and interpretive analysis. The researchers themselves are the main 'research instrument' and subjectivity and reflexivity tend to be privileged. Although social work researchers share many of these commitments, often insufficient attention is paid to the complexities of methodological positions and debates, leading to tendencies to rely unduly on knowledge derived from small, localized research studies which tell us little about outcomes, do not enable generalization, and so are often of limited utility. However, there is potential for qualitative approaches to counter these criticisms where method is taken seriously. We will explore these issues in more depth via discussion of the characteristics of research methods associated with particular paradigms.

Positivism

Experimental method has historically been closely associated with positivism. Recently, evidence-based practice has brought it back to the fore in social work as a seemingly useful way of producing objective evidence regarding the effectiveness of intervention. Critiques of these developments reflect the more long-standing critique of positivism (Smith 1979, 2002,) particularly by interpretivists regarding objectivist tendencies, the downplaying of individualized subjectivity and the seductive promise of science as a means of overcoming uncertainty.

Certain strengths arguably accrue to these methods, including the potential to establish relations of causality, replication, and prediction. As we have seen, their suitability in the social sciences has been a controversial issue, given that social life does not ordinarily closely resemble the controlled environment of the laboratory and so the extent to which it can actually be used as intended is lessened. Claims of replicability and predictive capacity are therefore limited, given that even experiments which have been particularly successful often fail to produce knowledge which is widely applicable. Interpretivists suggest that this is because experimental method does not take into account the variable meaning that the same situation will have for different individuals. In addition, there has been much discussion of the ethics of randomization (where intervention is provided to some service users but not to others) in research which seeks to specify treatment effect, while claims of objectivity are arguably false because value judgements are involved in deciding that a particular issue actually warrants investigation. There is also concern that the nature of experimental method is such that questions of cause and effect in social problems become individualized, with contextualizing social factors disregarded. In any case, it is argued, those who make decisions on the basis of the knowledge generated by these methods – 'evidence-based' policy-makers – often do not wait until the evidence is actually 'in', or disregard 'evidence' which is politically problematic. It is politics rather than evidence which determines the 'value' of a knowledge claim.

Interpretivism

In contrast with the focus in positivism on the pursuit of objectivity via bias minimization, here the role of subjective beliefs, values and opinions are seen as significant in themselves. If meaning – or knowledge – is made through interaction between individuals in social settings, then knowledge is not a representation of some essential, underpinning reality, but a socially constructed phenomenon which varies according to contingent, and highly individualized, factors. The quest for universally applicable laws which govern behaviour is therefore misplaced. Everitt et al. therefore argue that 'the only honest way forward...is for subjective meanings and experiences to be incorporated into the process of getting to know' (1992: 104).

Interpretive researchers are not concerned with establishing the nature and extent of relationships between variables, and regard the generalized data produced by positivists as constructions rather than facts. Instead they undertake in-depth interviews and ethnographic observation to elicit individualized, storied narratives which demonstrate how perceptions and understandings have effect in the lived reality of social relationships.

Such approaches are familiar to practitioners and many see congruence between interpretivism and social work values, given that both focus on bringing relatively neglected perspectives to the fore. However, their disregard for matters of causation, small sample sizes which limit external validity, and their reliance on subjectivity in interpretation of results prompt scepticism. In response interpretivists suggest that such lofty ambitions are beyond 'science' anyway, and that what differentiates interpretivism from positivism is a willingness to acknowledge as much.

Post-modernism

There are affiliations between interpretivism and post-modernism. Post-modernism challenges teleological narratives of progress via scientific discovery, and is sceptical about the status and wider applicability of modernist knowledge claims (Alvesson 2002). In place of a quest for certainty, 'all knowledge is relative and uncertain' (Corby 2006: 52). Post-modernism has influenced social work research in various ways, including by challenging taken-for-granted assumptions and grand claims associated with scientific modernity, and by challenging dominant ways of thinking via its emphasis on the multiplicity and fluidity of truth. Such research tends to be 'critically reflexive' and focused on the constituting effects of discourse, using deconstruction to highlight that which knowledge claims seek to disguise (Fawcett 2009).

Philosophically and ethically, then, within interpretivism there is a commitment to incorporating informal varieties of research knowledge, which are often given short shrift by dogmatic versions of positivism. Despite their strengths, though, these types of data are not particularly useful when seeking to assess the effectiveness of practice, given their emphasis on meaning rather than outcomes, and so they neglect a key contemporary challenge for social work.

Critical research

The particular distinctiveness of critical social research relates to its relationship with social movements concerned with emancipation and social change. Researchers seek to investigate and challenge the sources of social division by exposing structures and strategies which sustain unequal social and economic arrangements. It is assumed that these are underpinned by relations of domination and so the aim is to expose and change these. Understanding how relations of power are established and maintained via ideological and hegemonic processes, and resisted, are key concerns. Often, this is done by focusing on a particular institution or practice and subjecting its taken-for-granted assumptions to sustained critique, with emphasis on the role of political and historical context and processes. Common methodologies include in-depth qualitative interviewing, and observation and discursive analysis of official documents and statistics. Analytic strategies tend to be explanatory rather than descriptive or interpretive. There is a concern to ensure that knowledge has a change-related effect, and so the notion of praxis – knowledge as a basis for action – is key.

There is also emphasis on what the researcher brings to the research enterprise. Those researchers informed by critical theory will seek to analyse, deconstruct and challenge their own taken-for-granted, common-sense views and actions by identifying contextual influences, and thinking through how these impact upon their underpinning assumptions. By disentangling the relationships between actions, our assumptions and the influence of wider structural factors, the relationship between knowledge and power is foregrounded.

Critical perspectives inform anti-oppressive research which has certain key characteristics, including treating respondents 'as people and not as objects' (McLaughlin 2007: 129) via collaborative and participatory approaches. These can enable access to the experiences and perspectives of the oppressed. There is emphasis on explanations which accommodate the interaction between history, culture and society and the role of power. Emancipatory aims ensure linkages with approaches to undertaking research which are sympathetic to standpoint perspectives, such as participatory and action research. McLaughlin (2009) provides useful discussions of these approaches.

Critical research has itself been critiqued. It assumes that the nature of the relationship between service user and practitioner-researcher is generally consensual, which, given the statutory responsibilities social workers have in relation to risk, protection and vulnerability, can be problematic. There is also a concern that much critical research is highly theoretical, with disproportionate concern directed at abstract intellectual debates about the relationship between theory, practice and power, at the expense of practical activities which actually make a difference to the people experiencing the effects of social divisions. There is also the question of why, if your objective is social change, you would get involved in research rather than practice or activism in any case? Why do research at all when there are other, potentially more 'hands on' ways of working for change?

As critical research tends to be partisan, issues of objectivity and generalizability are bypassed. Given that social problems are constructed and responded to politically, and that service users often have very little influence within these debates, it is arguably right and proper that their experiences and knowledge are highlighted. Critical approaches offer the potential for this to occur directly, rather than being filtered through the familiar mechanisms of traditional research, which have evident limitations. Giving 'freedom to voice' to 'speak truth to power', however assumes that service user perspectives are homogeneous. In reality, they are likely to be variable. Equally, it may be that user perspectives are problematic for practitioners especially where issues of risk or vulnerability are foregrounded.

The principal, and probably most apt, criticism directed against research undertaken within a critical paradigm, then, is its partisan nature, which makes issues of the 'quality' of its knowledge claims difficult to assess. In bypassing concerns that ideological preferences may bias research outcomes, researchers lay themselves open to the criticism that their knowledge claims are not robust, and indeed, that their research 'discovers' what they want it to discover. Put another way, one's commitments affect one's judgement.

Are objectivity and partisanship compatible? Clearly not. By definition, they are polar opposites. The critical response, however, is powerful. Not only is partisanship compatible with its wider commitments, all research, including that which claims to be objective, is actually partisan to some extent. The notion of neutrality in social science is an idealized myth. Hammersley (1995), though, is unconvinced and has suggested that it must be the plausibility and credibility of evidence cited in support of research findings that is used as a basis for determining the veracity which is attached to a knowledge claim. Properly understood, research is a vehicle for knowledge generation, rather than a means of furthering political ends, and our commitments must be amenable to amendment in light of convincing contrary evidence – 'changing one's mind', as Sheldon and Macdonald (1998) put it. This is not a perspective shared by those who adhere to ideological positions come what may.

A midway position between that of Hammersley and the explicitly partisan leanings of wholly emancipatory positions is advocated by Shaw and Gould (2001). They take issue with the suggestion that partisan positions necessarily lead to concern about methodological rigour and relevance, suggesting that there is still scope for evaluating the rigour and relevance of knowledge claims by reference to criteria other than pre-existing values and commitments. Both the strong critique of standpoint perspectives, which argues that partisan positions compromise the validity of research findings, and the counter argument that participatory, user-led research is both morally and methodologically superior by virtue of the transparency of its social and political objectives are rejected. The latter is seen as indicative of undue 'sentimentality and romanticism' (2001: 175). The issue for social work research is where the line is drawn in relation to control of the agenda for research, and who draws it. The division on this issue tends to reflect positions regarding the nature and objectives of social work, which remain contested.

Realist research

Various authors have recently sought to demonstrate the relevance of the realist paradigm to social work research. Though principally concerned with evaluation, realist enquiry can be regarded as a form of research which is potentially useful in unpicking the relations between theory, practice and outcomes in social work.

Key in the development of this approach is the work of Pawson and Tilley (1996, 1997) who have specified an influential conceptual framework in which 'mechanisms', 'contexts' and 'outcomes' are highlighted. The first of these refers to the assumption that human behaviour occurs within social systems. As such, behaviour can only be made sense of by reference to wider social rules and institutions which effect decisions and actions. Because of this, notions of straight-forward cause and effect relationships between variables are seen as overly deterministic. Instead, attention must be paid to the 'wider web of expectations' (1996: 407) which are also impacting, including the background, experiences and aspirations of the people involved. Underlying generative 'mechanisms', which are assumed to be present even though they may not be observable, are key. Causal links are reformulated as descriptive rather than explanatory, requiring explanation themselves, via analysis of generative mechanisms. This represents a move away from asking whether an approach to practice achieves its aims in seeking to specify what it is about an approach that makes it work. The question here is not 'what works'?, but instead 'what works for whom, in what context, and why'?

Realists assume that there is inevitably a 'weaving process' which binds together decisions and actions, mechanisms and contexts. Contexts are inherently fluid and so the impact of a particular intervention will vary positively or negatively. Accurate prediction is therefore problematized. The interaction between mechanism and context in determining the outcome of interventions is the principal focus for the realist researcher. Context–mechanism–outcome configurations, represented in the formula 'Outcome = Mechanism + Context', are key.

Both empirical and qualitative research methods may be useful given the positioning of realism as separate from, but informed by, both positivism and interpretivism. Kazi asserts that 'Realism transcends the qualitative and quantitative divide, or the epistemological divide between empirical and interpretivist approaches' (2003: 6). Explanations entail empirical components, albeit in ways which are sympathetic to notions of contingency. This is a post-positivist approach, incorporating aspects of scientific method and philosophy, adapted to accommodate aspects of the interpretivist and critical critique.

Empirical and interpretivist methods are seen as useful for producing knowledge which is 'foundational', but falling short in attempts to explain the inner workings of an intervention – *why* it works. They do not adequately address links, and this is where realism may be useful. Thus knowledge about the effect of an intervention, which is produced empirically, via a randomized control trial, for example, is not regarded as an end in itself, but as a social fact requiring explanation by reference to underlying generative mechanisms. The goal is 'an explanation of an explanation' (Kazi 2003: 138). This type of explanatory knowledge is not produced inductively or deductively, but retroductively, which entails some combination of both alternatives. Objectivity and subjectivity are combined. In seeking to explain the impact of social work practice, intervention would be conceptualized as 'a mechanism that is introduced to effect change in a constellation of other mechanisms and structures, embedded in the context of pre-existing historical, economic, cultural, social and other conditions' (ibid.: 24). It is 'how' practice 'works' which realism seeks to claim as its own.

Of course realism has limitations. These are to do with, among other things, generalizability. According to realists, when something 'works', it does so because of a unique configuration of context and mechanism, which means it is very difficult to generalize similar configurations to other potential practice sites. Indeed, its awareness of the sheer complexity of the inter-relationship between multiple variables would seem to call into question the possibility of ever transferring what is known from one context to another, and – in extreme versions – render attempts to develop a professional knowledge base redundant. 'Soft' realism meanwhile puts limits on the extent to which research knowledge can answer generalized questions or resolve big challenges. It suggests that what we can know has limits. Nevertheless, its cyclical process (the 'realist evaluation cycle') means that in situated contexts it is possible to gradually get 'closer' to 'the answer'. The claim is that realism is therefore better placed to enable replication of positive intervention effects than alternative approaches.

Being methodologically pluralist and pragmatic, realism is vulnerable to criticism on two fronts. While realists seek to make a strength of their positioning and see no difficulty in unproblematically accommodating designs and methods derived from alternative perspectives, this 'strength' paradoxically leaves it open to criticism on the grounds that the limitations of each remain pertinent, but are compounded by their disregard for what strong advocates might regard as necessary commitments to underpinning philosophy. Kazi, however, argues that 'methods in themselves are not decisive; rather it is the perspective of the enquirer which determines how the methods are used, and for what purpose' (2003: 167). This pragmatism enables researchers to develop a deeper understanding than alternative frameworks, and thus is better equipped to generate knowledge with the capacity to improve practice.

Mixed-method research (pragmatism)

Of course, there are many in social work who do not trouble themselves with methodological and philosophical debate and are concerned with 'getting the job done'. The same can be said for research, where pragmatists suggest that epistemological debates are rarely fruitful as they cannot be resolved. Concerns about coherence between paradigm and method are considered redundant. What matters is that the research design and method adopted are suitable and feasible to answer the question to hand. 'Mixed-methods', in which different designs and techniques are combined, are arguably inevitable as a means of seeking to address the limitations of one approach by drawing on the strengths of another. They offer the potential to avoid philosophical dead ends which are resolvable only within their own terms of reference. Arguably, mixed-method approaches are inherently more likely to produce useful knowledge than 'stand-alone' methods. They are therefore better placed to ensure that understanding of the relationship between variables (intervention, service user and outcome) are accompanied by understanding of the influence of contextual factors.

Unsurprisingly, such approaches attract criticism. Humphries (2008), for example, regards mixed-method research not as a pragmatic attempt to answer research objectives and questions effectively but as another means via which positivist assumptions have come to dominate the practice of research. This is because efforts to minimize threats to internal validity are premised upon the belief that internal validity is possible, which assumes that there is a fixed reality which research data may reflect.

Others regard such debate – particularly allegations of incommensurability – as either practically irrelevant or unnecessarily polarized. In relation to research then, it is perfectly possible for interpretivists to use quantitative, and positivists qualitative data. Each has strengths and weaknesses, and these can be maximized and minimized via their combination. To be sure, this leads to some tensions – but there are tensions already, and if results are usefully employed, these can be left to members of what Becker (1993) refers to as the profession of 'philosophical and methodological worry'.

There are strengths and limitations associated with research conducted within all of the paradigms we have discussed. These render each more or less useful in relation to certain types of problem or question. Thus, for example, empirical methods may be suited to assessing intervention outcomes via quantification, interpretive approaches may be valuable in understanding the perceptions of participants, critical approaches have potential where the objective is action, rather than knowledge for its own sake, and realism claims to offer the potential to bridge the divide between these alternative perspectives. It is worth exploring the implications of this diverse scene for practitioners. In practical terms, how can social workers make sense of contested knowledge?

Exercise

Identify the strengths and limitations of the research strategies and methods associated with each paradigmatic position. Which of the various options do you regard as most likely to produce knowledge which is useful for practice, and why?

Critically appraising research

Against a backdrop in which the nature and purposes of knowledge are contested, it is arguably crucial that practitioners are able to identify, and understand the implications of, the assumptions underpinning research studies, and that they are able to integrate such understanding within attempts to establish the quality and utility of research to practice. Consequently there has recently been much emphasis on ensuring that social workers are able to critically evaluate knowledge claims arising from research. Two components – assessing quality and using knowledge – are central to ambitions that practice be knowledge based. As Sheppard puts it, 'professionals cannot just be in the business of applying knowledge. They need to be able to appraise that knowledge as well' (2004: 10). This is the purpose of critical appraisal which entails practitioners assessing the quality, appropriateness and relevance of knowledge claims using quality criteria as a basis for maximizing the positive potential of their work.

In relation to research knowledge, there are established, generic means of appraising the quality of findings which remain potentially useful for practitioners seeking to differentiate knowledge claims. Additionally, the use of critical appraisal 'tools' as a means of assessing the quality of knowledge claims has become much more significant recently. Various tools and checklists are available, which represent 'shortcuts' to assist practitioners in 'deciding whether or not to use particular research findings to inform decision-making within practice' (Newman et al. 2006: 56). Those who advocate such tools appear confident that practitioners are on the one hand in need of such assistance – often because of pressures of time – but also retain discretion to make decisions regarding courses of action.

Newman et al. (2006) acknowledge that critical appraisal tools cannot definitively differentiate high quality useful research knowledge, but nevertheless assert that they represent a workable means of operationalizing the principles of quality appraisal to assess trustworthiness in a user-friendly manner. Principally, this entails using the hierarchy of knowledge as a means of judging the likely veracity of findings, paying attention to research design, methods and analysis, and any attempts to limit or counter pre-existing preferences or bias via techniques such as data triangulation or respondent validation. This process is described as 'sorting the wheat from the chaff'. Although exemplars are provided which are suitable for studies which do not meet the criteria for rigour common in experimental research, positivist assumptions are arguably nevertheless embedded within the process.

This is also the case in the checklist of questions which Sheldon and Macdonald (2009) specify as a means of making quality judgements regarding knowledge. They assert that values and ethical commitments should be subordinate to a concern with establishing 'what works, for whom, at what cost, in what circumstances, over what time scale, against which outcome indicators, how, and why?' (2009: 89). Their 'basic questions' that practitioners can use to assess the quality of knowledge claims focus upon whether research questions are sufficiently specific to lend themselves to testing and falsification, and the strengths and weaknesses of the designs and methods used for this purpose. Criteria include the size and representativeness of samples and their implications for external validity, the adequacy of outcome measures, their statistical significance, and the implications of these for practice relevance. They also urge that practitioners be alert to the potential for hopes and aspirations to skew the analysis of data and representation of findings and guard against the effects of 'weasel words' which disguise the limitations of a particular study.

Sheppard's (2004) framework for critical appraisal is straight-forward. It specifies four main questions (and various subsidiaries) that may be asked about a knowledge claim by practitioners. Firstly, what kind of assumptions does a piece of research embody? (i.e. what are the paradigmatic affiliations of the researcher? Are these stated, or can they be inferred?). Second, how well has the research been undertaken? (Are the methods used, with their particular strengths and weaknesses, appropriate to the question they are seeking to address? Do they do this well?). Next, how useful is the research, and finally, in what ways might it be applicable? This approach entails a 'focusing' down of attention away from the holistic 'whole' to those aspects of a case which are most urgent or relevant and potentially enables meaningful integration between knowledge and practice. It has potential for establishing whether or not we should heed the claims of a particular piece of research.

The generic quality standards which SCIE advocate (TAPUPAS) seeks to make such judgements more relevant by ensuring that the criteria which are used to assess a knowledge claim are specific to the source from which it is derived. In relation to research knowledge, there is a need to be responsive to 'the particularly broad church of perspectives and paradigms' (2003: 26) of which social work research is comprised. Here, the veracity of the hierarchy of knowledge is challenged by the assumption that all of these are of equal potential value. However, the development of TAPUPAS in the first place is indicative of a belief that criteria are required to assist in determining whether knowledge claims are relevant and useful in a particular situation, and that these are not self-evident. What is not specified are criteria against which elements of TAPUPAS should be measured or applied. Though not advocating infinite regress, it is surely the case that practitioners will need to rely on subjective judgement here.

Optimistically, then, this represents a statement of confidence in the capabilities and competence of social workers to bring their professionalism to bear in assessing knowledge claims.

Exercise

Critical appraisal asks that practitioners ask a number of questions regarding knowledge claims. Review the articles by Bradshaw (2003) and Kim and Fox (2006) considered in Chapter 2. Answer the following questions:

What are the major claims made in these accounts?
What are the paradigmatic affiliations of the authors?
What are the strengths and limitations of the methods used and the knowledge generated?

Now use the critical thinking tools identified in the exercise in Chapter 2 to evaluate Bradshaw (2003) and Kim and Fox (2006). References for these articles are in the reference section and the tools can be downloaded from www.ripfa.org.uk/aboutus/archive/skills.asp? TOPcatsubID=4&id=4

Critical appraisal, then, asks that practitioners identify the underpinning assumptions of a knowledge claim – its paradigmatic affiliations – and/or its source and assess its quality – its strengths and weaknesses – using the criteria appropriate for a specific paradigm, method or source. What is evident, however, is that even here there is a divergence of views regarding the ethics and practicalities of this task, which (to labour the point) arguably reflect the paradigmatic preferences of proponents of different tools. As such, critical appraisal does not resolve such disputes, rather it operationalizes them.

The limits of research in practice

The assumption underpinning contemporary commitments to embedding research skills in practice is that social work is enhanced as a result. However, though useful in some respects, there are various tensions which render this less than straightforward. It is important, therefore, that research skills are seen as supplementing, rather than replacing, other key skills, including clinical judgement and reflection.

It would be a mistake to assume that practice will automatically be of a higher quality if it is better integrated with research. As McLaughlin puts it, 'Research tends to complicate issues by making them more complex to reflect reality while practitioners and policy-makers are more concerned with simplifying things so that action becomes possible' (2007: 153). Researchers and social workers are concerned with knowledge development and application, respectively. There are parallels between the two enterprises, but they are not one and the same. Research does not solve the problems of practice, precisely because research and practice are separate enterprises. There is a need to 'dispel the myth that research has the answer to practice problems in the form that practitioners may require' (Corby 2006: 167). This is necessary because of the acknowledged limitations of social research in providing 'answers', or courses of action to choose between and act upon, in all of the myriad of situations with which practitioners are confronted. Often, knowledge is pitched generally, which makes its application at the level of the individual difficult. Equally, it may be couched in terms of probabilities (particularly where risk is a concern) which mean that associated courses of action do not necessarily 'apply' to a particular service user. Alternatively, it may derive from a study which is similar to the situation with which we are presented, but also different, and so its direct relevance may be limited. In such circumstances, it would be unduly optimistic to imagine that 'research knowledge' can be the primary basis for practice. Instead, it offers us 'information that can help provide guidance, and better informed judgements, but not certainty' (Sheppard 2004: 23). This is much more realistic. All research has strengths and limitations in practice which reflect its underpinning assumptions and which criteria of quality and utility have been adhered to. As activities, however, research and practice interact, and there is scope for this to be a constructive liaison.

5

Understanding Policy Frameworks

Understanding policy frameworks is a key professional requirement of social work training and practice. As a social worker you are required to: 'Review and update your own knowledge of legal, policy and procedural frameworks' (TOPSS 2002:18.1) and to 'Contribute to policy review and development' (ibid.: 21.1). Policy knowledge is an essential element in the armoury of professional skills, and can provide a key resource for advocacy in social work. The START Project in Plymouth, for instance, is a student unit working with refugee families. One aspect of its work is the use of policy knowledge and advocacy skills by students in placement to enable people to access services (Butler 2005, 2007). For example:

> Mrs F, who spoke very little English, had complained consistently of stomach pain to the GP surgery where she was seen as an attention-seeking nuisance. The student's perseverance in advocating for her right to translation provision resulted in an emergency examination and immediate admission to hospital for treatment of a neglected life-threatening infection. (Butler 2005:151)

The student was aware that 'The NHS plan set the target of free and nationally available translation service from all NHS services via NHS Direct by 2003' (Butler 2008) and used this policy knowledge to ensure that local services recognized Mrs F's rights.

This chapter looks at social work's relationship with policy knowledge. One approach would be to describe the policies relevant to social workers. However, there is no uniform set of policies that applies to all social work practice; policies apply in different ways to different areas of social work practice in different places. In terms of policy, social work is a fragmented discipline. For instance, a fundamental distinction now exists between 'children and families' and 'adult care' as areas of social work practice:

> in response to the Children Act 2004...education and social care services for children will be brought together under a director of children's services in each local authority. Adult social services will be delivered via a director for adult services, which replaces the current director of social services role. (Every Child Matters 2008)

Social work in the UK has always been carried out within different policy and legislative frameworks – between national boundaries, and between authorities within the different nations (Hill 2000b, 2003). In the wake of devolution, social workers operate within increasingly different policy contexts in Wales, Scotland, Northern Ireland and England (Critical Social Policy 2006); and analysts point to divergence in policy commitments between the four nations. Greer, for instance, notes that 'In the short time since devolution there has been surprising policy divergence and even greater divergence in the values and "mood music" of the four systems. Even the shibboleths now vary: England speaks of "modernization", Wales of "inequalities" and even (quietly) "socialism", Scotland of "partnership".' (Greer 2003: 212). See Box 5.1 on page 99.

In the following section we will first look at what policy is, and the nature of policy that relates to social work practice. Policy covers a range of ideas and activities, but in practice it relates to the guidance, regulations and structures within which social workers carry on their day-to-day work. There are different ideas about the way social workers work with policy. One emphasizes policy as fixed, clear and precise rules, which practitioners simply need to know and follow. The other portrays policy as more complex and sees practitioners as making sense and practical use of it at ground level. A central idea here is that of professional discretion, in terms of both the freedom to make decisions and the exercise of judgement this decision-making involves. In the remainder of this chapter we will explore each of these issues in turn.

What is policy?

Policy knowledge crosses the boundaries of politics, administration and practice. It denotes both strategic commitments and a practical

Box 5.1

The following websites are the key sources of information for social care policy across the four nations of the UK.

England
Adult social care
Department of Health (DoH):
http://www.dh.gov.uk/en/SocialCare/Deliveringadultsocialcare/index.htm
Children and families:
Department for Children, Schools and Families: http://www.dcsf.gov.uk/
'Every child matters': http://www.everychildmatters.gov.uk/socialcare/

Northern Ireland Government
Department for Health, Social Services and Public Safety (DHSSPS NI)
Child care: http://www.dhsspsni.gov.uk/index/hss/child_care.htm
Adult community care: http://www.dhsspsni.gov.uk/index/hss/ec-community-care.htm

The Scottish Government
Adult social care: http://www.scotland.gov.uk/Topics/Health/care
Children and young people: http://www.scotland.gov.uk/Topics/People/Young-People

Llywodraeth Cynulliad Cymru | The Welsh Assembly Government
Children and young people: http://new.wales.gov.uk/topics/childrenyoungpeople/careandprotection/?lang=en
Adult social care: http://new.wales.gov.uk/topics/health/socialcare/adultsocialservices/?lang=en

Exercise
Looking at policy in different countries can help you think about other ways of working. For instance, the Welsh Assembly Government first developed the role of Children's Commissioner, which was recently introduced in England. Take a look at a website from another part of the UK and consider ways in which the policies are similar to and different from the policies in your own country.

plan of action. Pawson et al., for instance, note that policy knowledge '...ranges from the profession of broad principles to underpin social services (for example, from "welfare to well-being"), to suggestions for structural models to deliver them (for example, "public-private partnerships"), to the promotion of implementation strategies (for example, "user and carer involvement")'. (Pawson et al. 2003: 53)

Politicians and senior officials tend to talk about policy in different ways (Levine 1997): as an intention to make changes; and as the way in which services are currently organized and delivered. Policy may refer to custom and practice, the ways in which services have traditionally been conducted or provided. It is also used as a 'trump card' – the official and approved way of acting: for instance, government policy is to modernize services. Levine (ibid.) argues that, underpinning the differences, it is possible to see basic similarities that give the idea of policy common characteristics. Policy is a commitment; an intention to continue with a situation or to change something in the real world; policy also belongs to someone – the government, the council, the team etc. – implying a claim that it should be acted on and followed by those whom it covers; and finally policy, as a practical programme, is more than a vague sense that something should be done: it has sufficient clarity to enable organizations, professional groups and individual workers to convey what they are being asked to do.

Policy, then, refers both to commitments and to a detailed programme of action which seeks to put strategic commitments into effect. The Modernising Government White Paper, for instance, talks about policy-making as a 'process by which governments translate their political vision into programmes and actions to deliver "outcomes" – desired changes in the real world' (Cabinet Office 1999: ch. 2 para. 1).

Policy necessarily straddles both political and administrative worlds because ministers and their officials have to rely on others – agencies, councils, professionals etc. – to carry out policies on the ground (Levine 1997). They direct local practices from the centre (Rhodes 1997, 2008), but '... pulling the central policy lever does not necessarily mean something happens at the bottom. Such frustrations lead to colourful language. So, for the Department of Health, instilling financial discipline in doctors is likened to "herding cats".' (Rhodes 2008: 1255)

As a social worker working with policy, one is not only engaging in a technical administrative task, but also working with political and ethical issues (Drakeford 2002). Policy embodies the goals and commitments of politicians and officials in decision-making centres such as central government departments in London, the devolved governments in Cardiff, Edinburgh and Belfast and different levels in local authorities and other public agencies. Policy has often percolated through several political levels before it reaches street level, and has been the subject of argument, dispute and compromise. It is '...often rhetorical or speculative: "As politicians know only too well, but social scientists too often forget, public policy is made of language. Whether in written or oral form, argumentation is central to all stages of the policy process."' (Pawson et al. 2003: 53).

Implementing policy

Social work practice is often discussed as if it occurs in vacuum, when in fact it takes place within organizations (White and Harris 2007). Social work is organized within the policy of the agency; but practitioners' decisions also influence how policy works and what it means at street level (Evans and Harris 2004). As a practitioner you are concerned with putting policies into effect – for instance the Common Assessment Frameworks in Children's services and in Adult services; but how you put policy into effect – how you use the framework – *becomes* the public policy, and has more impact on the day-to-day lives of services users than formal policy statement (Lipsky 1980).

This raises fundamental questions about social work and policy work.

- What policy knowledge do practitioners require? What sources of information, in addition to policy documents, tell us what policy is on the ground?
- How do social workers relate to formal policy in practice? What is the role of professional discretion in implementing policy and what impact does discretion have on the relationship between policy knowledge and practice?

Where's the policy?

Exercise

On your first week in placement how would you find out which policies apply in your work setting? Where would you look? Who would you ask?

While we need to be aware of general statements and political vision, when we talk about policy in relation to social work practice, we're primarily talking about translating these broad statements into practical programmes of work.

Over the past few decades central government has increasingly sought to control more directly the local implementation of policy (e.g. Timmins 1995; Rhodes 1997, 2008). A primary tool in this regard has been the increase of managerial strategies, which have sought to stipulate what services should look like and to monitor and control their delivery in line with these stipulations.

Levine (1997) identifies four broad approaches taken by government to translate policy into practice through implementation.

1 The law. Laws give local authorities powers and impose on them duties to deliver services. Another aspect of this form of control is the use of procedures to specify the interpretation of law, and what particular duties and powers entail.

2 Government influence on service organization. For instance, the establishment of social services departments in England and Wales in the 1970s was a clear policy decision to give social care a priority in local government services.

3 Government influence on service management. This can range from appointing senior posts to changing the nature of the workforce and monitoring and regulating performance against established standards – for instance, the establishment of the Performance Assessment Framework for local authority social services (see Box 5.2 on page 103).

4 Funding. Since the 1980s the amount of funding given to local authorities to provide services has become increasingly dependent on central government. The vast majority of their budgets comes from this source, and this is supplemented by the local community charge and charges made for services (Rhodes 1997; Hill 2000a). Central government's tools for influencing local authorities (and other agencies) are not simply instructions from above, but also include transactions such as payment for services as a means of encouraging service provision (Rhodes 1997, Hill 2003). Furthermore, these tools do not exist in isolation. They have to build on what has gone before, and to interact with policy in other areas.

Box 5.2   Practice and Performance Assessment Frameworks

In Modernising Social Services (1998) the government set out its aim to assess and compare the performance of all social services. Performance Assessment Frameworks are now used to measure the performance of services against set standards such as (for adults) 'better health and well-being', 'making a positive contribution'. Local services are then rated on a four-point scale from 'no star' (poor) to 'three stars' (excellent). Ofsted now produces performance tables for children's services: http://www.ofsted.gov.uk/portal/site/Internet/menuitem.eace3f09a603f6d9c3172a8a08c08a0c/?vgnextoid=5149f32414804110VgnVCM1000003507640aRCRD

The Care Quality Commission assesses adult social care: http://www.cqc.org.uk/guidanceforprofessionals/socialcare.cfm.

The way social workers practise can influence league tables. It is important not only to do a good job but to make sure the paperwork is completed in the right way, as this social worker explains:

> The PAF indicators get checked very regularly and we get feedback from people that deal with our stats…There's extra pressure on that at the moment; our PAF indicators led to us being named and shamed. So we want to improve that, which is fair enough. But sometimes the professional bit doesn't seem to fit too squarely with the paperwork. [The team manager] says it does, but it doesn't quite feel right to me sometimes.[1]

Box 5.3   Individual Budgets: Funding, Choice and Empowerment

Brian Collinge, an ex local authority chief executive, is concerned that if individual budgets are '…introduced in an atmosphere of severe financial constraints, as pertains at present, and used as an instrument of cost reduction, the results could be very damaging' (Brindle 2008: 5).

Andrew Cozens, Strategic Adviser for Children, Adults and Health Services at the Improvement and Development Agency for Local Government, sees individualized budgets as running in parallel with 'the principle of co-payment or topping-up state-funded entitlement…' (Cozens 2008: 6).

Reflective Questions: Thinking about your local area, will individual budgets give choice and empowerment equally to everyone who uses adult services?

---

[1] All unattributed practitioner quotes that follow are taken from research published in Evans, T. (2010) *Professional Discretion in Welfare Services*, Aldershot: Ashgate.

Examples of this complexity can be found throughout social work areas. Look, for instance, at the current implementation of 'Every Child Matters' (DES 2003). A key piece of legislation putting this policy into effect is the Children Act 2004. However, in relation to social care, the main statutory basis for services to children continues to be the 1989 Children Act. What the 2004 Act does is change the way in which services are provided. It has now separated off social care for children and families from social care for adults, providing children's services alongside education within local authorities and changing the structure of service delivery. In implementing Every Child Matters and the 2004 Children Act, the government has provided a plethora of guidance and advice, including statutory guidance which local authorities are duty-bound to note; but also documents and resources which seek to persuade local authorities and professionals to change their practices and operate more in accordance with the government's vision.

Implementing policy

There are two broad approaches to policy, knowledge and practice. These are not hard and fast categories but distinctions that can help you to think about how you as a social worker relate to and respond to policy.

- The 'top-down' approach characterizes policy as *instructions*. According to this approach, policy is a clear blueprint that social workers need to know, so that they can put it into effect. Policy knowledge is contained in procedures and guidelines. This approach entails recognition that, as a practitioner, one is obliged to obey policy directives.
- The 'bottom-up' approach sees policy as complex and uncertain. Policy needs to be interpreted, prioritized and translated into practice, using professional judgement and discretion. Here practitioners are seen less as consumers of policy than as active policy-makers at street level, who put policy in its broader political, social and ethical context.

In the remainder of this chapter we will consider what each of these approaches can tell us about the skills and knowledge required by social workers in their role as policy-implementers.

Top-down policy

The first approach sees social work's relationship to policy as passive. Practitioners implement policy and procedures as directed. 'Policy' is clear, authoritative, discrete and coherent. Practitioners implement predetermined policy that is controlled from the top (Hogwood and Gunn 1984). Policy knowledge for practice comes from the clear strategic vision provided by the top and comes down as instructions embodied in policy and procedures.

Practitioners are employed within the organization to carry out its policies and are accountable through its hierarchy for ensuring that their practice complies with the policy blueprint. An important concern of this approach is the possibility of mismatches between the strategic vision (the policy blueprint) and the practice and service delivery on the ground. This is described as 'the implementation gap', and sees implementation, rather than policy itself, as the problem. At ground level, this involves judging practice against the blueprint, and being suspicious of discretion.

In contemporary social services the top-down approach to policy implementation can be detected in the influence of managerialism within social work organizations:

> Effective organizations are seen as needing clear objectives resulting in quantifiable outcomes, requiring performance indicators and monitoring of performance against them, in order to decide whether they have been successful. Accordingly, New Labour has defined social work's objectives at national level, has set outcomes to be achieved locally and has monitored results. (White and Harris 2007:246)

From the 'top-down' perspective the nature of policy knowledge for practice is quite clear. It involves understanding the policy in terms of organizational instructions, policies and procedures. Problems arise when practitioners are unclear about their role and responsibilities, or when *they* muddy the waters by bringing in concerns and perspectives that are extraneous to their prescribed role within the organization.

Lewis and Glennerster, reviewing the literature on public policy implementation, observe that the 'top-down' view assumes: '...that, if not the local detail, then at least the broad intellectual rationale for the policy is tightly conceived by the centre' (Lewis and Glennerster 1996: 20). (For 'centre', read 'top'.) However, they see this assumption as, at best, highly questionable (ibid.: 20). Recent research examining the application of changing guidelines for community care services illustrates the problem of assuming that policy is a clear guide to practice. Bradley identifies '...insufficient clarity or openness in local procedures...coupled with local political and economic expediency...as significant factors in creating extensive discretion in application of charges for services among practitioners and managers' (Bradley 2003: 653).

The top-down perspective assumes that the authors of a policy can determine the way that policy is understood and interpreted at street level. Critics argue that policy, like any text, is not fully under the control of its authors. The intended content of any document (what the authors mean) is not necessarily the same as its received content (what the document's readers understand) (Scott 1990: 34). Policymakers often assume background values and ideas that policy-implementers do not necessarily share. Implementation studies often note local confusion and misunderstanding – 'puzzlement' – about what the centre is asking them to do (Harrison et al. 1992: 3–4; Preston-Shoot and Wigley 2002).

The preceding criticisms should not prevent us from recognizing two important insights associated with the top-down perspective: that the centre has policy positions and commitments; and that these policies have some authority: 'While attempts will subsequently be made by unconvinced local authorities and others "upon whom action depends" to modify and re-direct the policy's thrust, there are surely limits – if only legal and constitutional – to how far such post-legislative guerrilla skirmishing should take place' (Hogwood and Gunn 1984: 208).

Box 5.4   Policy and Practice at Ground Level

Read this comment from a practitioner about the experience of working with policies and consider these questions: Should professionals ignore some rules to get the job done or should they work by the book? Why might an agency encourage professionals to be flexible with policies?

'I think what happens a lot is that the written policies and procedures are almost over the top on the side of the worthiness and including everything under the sun and every consideration – in a way that is totally unrealistic, given the resources that are actually devoted to doing the assessments...You'd get through about two a week if you do them like that.'

Bottom-up policy work

In contrast to the 'top-down' view, the 'bottom-up' approach starts from the assumption that policy is complex, fragmented and a challenge to implementers, who have to make sense of it and make it work (Barret and Fudge 1981, Barret and Hill 1984). Putting policy into practice entails the active role of the practitioner, who has to employ judgement in filling in gaps, translating and interpreting policies, and deciding between conflicting policy priorities. The 'bottom-up' approach to policy and policy implementation requires a much broader understanding of the nature of policy knowledge and a different sense of how, in practice, we use knowledge. It presents policy as part of a wider nexus of other policies and concerns, and the product of an ongoing political process; it has to be carried out in a real-world setting of scarce resources. It also underlines the fact that policy relies on practitioners to make sense of it, and the need for a reflective awareness on the part of practitioners of the discretion they exercise as policy-makers (DofH 2007; Rhodes 1997, 2008).

Perhaps the most influential portrayal of the nature and challenges of the 'bottom-up' policy-making is Lipksy's account of street-level bureaucrats – and, for Lipsky (1980), social workers are classic street-level bureaucrats. He describes street-level bureaucrats working with inadequate resources and high caseloads: they have fragmented contact with clients and have to make rapid decisions, typically under conditions of limited time and information. The problem of resources – funding, time etc. – is compounded by often vague and wide-ranging organizational goals which are difficult to define: what, for instance, is a 'customer-centred service'? In an attempt to avoid this problem, organizations often produce further guidance and procedures. However, for Lipsky, such efforts are as likely to confuse the situation as to clarify it:

> It is desirable to clarify objectives if they are needlessly and irrelevantly fuzzy or contradictory. However, while agency goals may be unclear or contradictory for reasons of neglect and historical inertia, they may also be unclear or contradictory because they reflect the contradictory impulses of the society the agency serves. The dilemma for accountability is to know when goal clarification is desirable, because continued ambivalence and contradiction are unproductive, and when it will result in a reduction in the scope and mission of public services. (Lipsky 1980: 165)

In their day-to-day work street-level bureaucrats have to work out practical versions of public policy that can often look quite unlike official pronouncements. When such distortions of policy are 'discovered', workers can be castigated for thwarting policy intentions but Lipsky locates the problem at a structural level. He points out that the short cuts and policy distortions developed at street level are often tacitly accepted by managers as real-world solutions to getting the job done.

Discretion

Practitioners have a degree of freedom within their work role: 'A public officer has discretion whenever the effective limits on his [*sic*] power leave him free to make a choice among possible courses of action or inaction' (Davis 1971: 4). Management techniques to control the work of street-level bureaucrats are difficult to operate – it's impossible to define what a 'good' service is and there is the constant risk that imposing performance measures can distort service delivery (Lipsky 1980). Within this complex relationship between top-down bureaucratic control and day-to-day implementation, practitioners have to make decisions about what policy they will put into effect because: 'Policy does not come neatly tied up in sealed packages. It is made as people and organizations interpret it, translate it, try to make it meaningful within the frames of reference they bring to their work, and shape it in innovated ways' (DofH 2007: 106–7).

At the most basic level practitioners have to decide which policies to prioritize and which to ignore:

> there are so many rules and procedures and everything else that...you know, no-one's got the memory of an elephant, so everybody's got a whole load that they can't remember. So there's a sort of ignoring of certain things...And in a sense I think that's quite tolerated...

When policy is viewed in this way it gives rise to a very different idea of practitioners' role in policy implementation. Rather than having clear instructions to implement, they are faced with complex, often contradictory instructions that may be difficult to understand, and day-to-day resources that don't match the grand visions of policy rhetoric. As a result, policy is made at street level by the interaction of instructions, the prioritizing of conflicts and the tailoring of rhetoric to reality.

In the remainder of this chapter we will look at how practitioners make policy by bringing their own knowledge, perspectives and concerns into play in their exercise of discretion.

The spirit rather than the letter

Implementing policy raises questions about the practitioner's accountability as a street-level policy-maker. How should practitioners carry out their role as 'bottom-up' policy-makers? What expertise and knowledge should they draw on in carrying out this role?

One view is that practitioners should be policy entrepreneurs (Lipsky 1980). Making sense of policy often involves disregarding the letter of the policy to make it work. According to this view, the important thing is to ensure that compromises and adaptations of organizational policies and procedures are guided by a commitment to the spirit – the fundamental aims – of the policy. Indeed, policy-makers and managers often assume that procedures will not be followed to the letter, but that practitioners will use their judgement to make them work. This is clearly the message from the Chief Social Services Inspector in her exhortation to practitioners to use their discretion in implementing the government's modernization agenda: 'The changes require... A culture of care that engages with the hearts and minds, as well as the budgets, of all those involved. A culture of care, which knows that consistency is important but it has to be implemented with intelligence and enterprise, not dogma; a culture of care, which puts an end to checklists that replace thinking and judgement' (Social Services Inspectorate 2001: 8).

Political sense

An alternative approach is to use one's 'political antennae' in the use of discretion. This idea entails recognizing that policy is a political process and has a political aim. Policy comes about from a process of commitment, conflict, negotiation and compromise. As a result, policy is itself a political act; it does not always mean what it says, and some of the things it says are more important than others. Policy analysts have argued that policy statements need to be understood as having a 'core' – the key purpose, concern and actions – which is their fundamental purpose, while other elements are secondary: aspirations or just rhetorical flourishes (Sabatier 1986: 40–4). The fundamental core of policy, its basic principles, are non negotiable. Beyond these fundamental points – that is, in relation to '...most decisions concerning administrative rules, budgetary allocations, disposition of cases, statutory interpretation...' (ibid.: 43), practitioners learn that these are negotiable. Lewis and Glennerster used this framework to analyse community care reform in the 1990s. These reforms were presented as providing a more flexible and user-focused service by the government. However, authorities were largely left to their own devices in this aspect of the policy. The fundamental concern of the government, its core policy, was: 'the need to stop the haemorrhage in the social security budget and to do so in a way that would minimize political outcry and not give additional resources to the local authorities themselves. Most of the rest of the policy was for the birds' (Lewis and Glennerster 1996: 8).

According to this point of view, practitioners have to approach policy with a realistic political sense, identify its core purpose and focus on this, recognizing that other policy elements are not a priority, and that discretion to follow or ignore them is tacitly acknowledged. Here, for instance, a social worker reflects on his work in an older person's team: '...the must-do things is [sic] very much centred round money. Anything that causes a problem around money is a definite no-no! Getting expenditure properly authorized and things like that.'

Moral commitment

But what if the practitioner disagrees with the spirit of the policy or the 'core' political aim? Some commentators look outside policy and the political context for guidance on how to make sense of policy. Here, a commonly advocated approach is for professionals to look to their own moral commitments. For Banks, contemporary social work, particularly in the public sector, has to operate in an increasingly unsympathetic context. Social services organizations, influenced by managerial concerns, are striving to control and direct professional practice through the imposition of procedures, rules and policies. Accordingly, for Banks (2006), organizational rules require ethical evaluation, questioning and transforming agency practice in the light of ethical commitments.

Banks acknowledges a risk of individuals imposing their own personal values and beliefs, and consequently of favouritism or abuse of power. She argues that practitioners have a responsibility to follow a less personalized commitment to justice in the use of discretion, and that, in doing this, '...it is important that social work operates within an institutional framework of rights and duties, to protect both the social worker and the service user' (ibid.: 132).

Box 5.5

Should social workers follow policy regardless of professional principles? Should they seek to challenge or change policies with which they disagree? Read the following quotations from social workers struggling with these issues in their day-to-day work. Note your reactions to what they say.

'Going back to when I applied for my CCETSW training...I suppose I saw [social work] in terms of empowering people and facilitating and advocating for people...And I still see those roles as being relevant. But working, for instance, in the kind of field I'm working in now, with...older people and increased eligibility criteria...you're limited in some things you can do, so you become a bit more of a sort of agent of social control, in a way

...it almost seems that the whole job gets subsumed into carrying out the authority's instructions...I find it disappointing how little resistance there is to a lot of things...There doesn't seem to be any sort of groundswell...it seems to me that part of our role is to be advising the authority as social workers about things and saying: you're employing us as professionals, not as dogsbodies...I don't think we do enough of that.'

In terms of the relationship between social work and policy, this argument raises a fundamental issue of democratic accountability, which is at the core of the top-down argument against discretion in policy implementation outlined above: what right have social workers, who are employed to implement policy, to change and make policy?

Another perspective sees professionals not as standing outside policy but as part of it: their role and discretion are, according to this view, based on the requirements of public policy; and they are authorized to act with a degree of freedom from external control in their work (Noon and Blyton 2000; Evetts 2002). They exercise their discretion '...both in respect of their professional judgements and decision-making, and in respect of their immunity from regulation or evaluation by others' (Evetts 2002: 341), and are given this discretionary role because the values they seek to advance, and are measured against, are recognized in policy as socially valuable. The GSCC (2008), the regulatory body for social work in England, for instance, identifies the promotion of social justice – and challenging injustices – as core roles in social work.

Box 5.6

Social work is defined by its core commitments. Public policy bodies, e.g. GSCC (2008) and BASW (2002), the professional body for social work in Britain, subscribe to the International Federation of Social Workers and the International Association of Schools of Social Work (2000) definition of social work:

'The social work profession promotes social change, problem-solving in human relationships and the empowerment and liberation of people to enhance well-being. Utilizing theories of human behaviour and social systems, social work intervenes at the points where people interact with their environments. Principles of human rights and social justice are fundamental to social work.'

As a social worker you have to act in accordance with standards of ethical professional practice – identified by regulatory bodies and your professional peers (see Box 5.6). The social worker's role, then, is itself a statement of public policy. While public officials have to be accountable and are expected to act justly by following the rules, there also exists within public services a suspicion of professionals who simply follow orders or who officiously follow procedures. Harris, for instance, has identified the danger of 'defensive practice in social work' in terms of denying the possibility of discretion, as a mode of self protection:

> instructions produced by local authorities often include not only mandatory procedures, but also rules of guidance. The latter can be departed from when good reasons can be adduced for doing so. A social worker who thought that it would be in the best interests of a client not to follow a guidance rule, but who decided to follow it all the same because he wanted to cover himself against any charge of negligence – by being able to claim that he was merely following authorized instructions – would be acting defensively. (Harris 1987: 65)

Conclusion

The ability to use policy to empower service users is a key aspect of professional social work practice. However, understanding and using policy involves social workers in a complex, contested and fragmented area of knowledge.

Policy knowledge in social work is complex because policy is 'decentred' and dynamic. The skills a social worker needs in working with policy involve recognizing its broad nature – not just procedures and policy statements, but also budgets, institutional arrangements and cultures of management etc.

Social workers tend to work in and through organizations, and a key aspect of their day-to-day work is as policy-implementers. One view is that policy is made at the top and handed down to practitioners to implement. Here, policy would be understood as instructions, and social workers would need only a clear idea of what these instructions say, in order to put them into effect. Another sees policy as a rickety framework within which practitioners must practise, and which they must interpret and adapt to local circumstances. This involves recognizing policy in its widest sense, as made up of procedures, institutional practices, funding, etc. Understanding policy in this way also highlights the role of professional judgement and decision-making as important elements of policy knowledge. Practitioners in this circumstance are faced with a need to understand their discretion – their freedom to make decisions, and adapt and develop policy in practice – and to reflect on the basis of this freedom and the way in which it is employed.

Three possible approaches have been considered. One is to look beyond the letter of policy, to recognize its underpinning principles, and to use that recognition to guide practice. A second is to develop a political sense of organizational priorities. These two approaches entail looking to policy for guidance. The third approach emphasizes professional values as the standard which guides the use of discretion. Here, an understanding of professional roles as themselves a dimension of policy underlines a legitimate and appropriate basis for informing and guiding professional policy practice.

6

Practitioner Knowledge

Authoritative voices such as SCIE are clear that practitioner knowledge is both inherent and necessary in social work. But what is actually distinctive about practitioner knowledge? Here, we outline the various components which cumulatively 'make up' practitioner knowledge, including formal, empirical knowledge and less scientific, informal, intuitive and tacit approaches. Utilizing the framework we have established earlier we explore the links between these different ways of 'thinking about thinking in practice' and established paradigmatic positions. We also pay particular attention to the tensions between 'art' and 'science' in social work.

The nature of knowledge in practice

Although SCIE specify practitioner knowledge as a distinctive form of knowledge which practitioners might utilize, it is itself arguably comprised of several different varieties of knowledge which are either seen as competing or complementary. A broad distinction is usually drawn between formal and informal knowledge. Formal knowledge can refer to theory or research, but also law or policy, while informal knowledge refers to practice wisdom, personal experience, intuition and tacit knowledge. There are debates regarding the relative status of these, particularly with regard to which should take precedence in contested scenarios. The suggestion is that the former align more readily with versions of practice which are 'scientific' while the latter are closer to 'art', being acknowledged as subjective rather than 'factual'. Whereas more generally there is a hierarchy, with formal knowledge regarded as more 'pure' than informal knowledge, arguably such distinctions do not hold in practice-based disciplines. This is the position taken by Wilson et al., who argue that practice represents 'a tangled web of knowledge' (2008: 99). As such, all forms should be treated as equally important, as complementary rather than competing. Although this may appear reasonable, it is actually a controversial position. Sheldon and Macdonald (2009) argue strongly that it is right and proper that hierarchies of knowledge are used as a basis for structuring the relationship between theory and practice. Gambrill (2006) and Thyer and Wodarski (2007) go further, arguing that a failure to do so represents unethical practice. Unsurprisingly, such allegations are rebutted.

Practice which draws upon formal knowledge, then, tends to be seen within some 'versions' of social work as more appropriate than that which does not. Practice theories – theories 'for' rather than 'of' social work – are not, however, fixed but evolve according to reflection on their utility in particular practice contexts, in a dynamic, reciprocal and mutually constituting fashion. Despite the 'hybrid' nature of resultant formulations, with formal and informal engaged in complex liaisons, nevertheless hierarchal relations are posited as preferable by some. The risk here is that knowledge which is of a nature or status which does not meet the requirements of such hierarchies, but which practitioners do find useful, or have no realistic option but to draw upon, is disregarded. Standing in opposition to such views are various forms of 'informal' knowledge.

Informal knowledge

Practice wisdom refers to knowledge or expertise which practitioners accumulate over time by virtue of their professional experience. By its nature, often this type of knowledge is implicit or unspoken – that is, tacit – though sometimes it may be shared among colleagues or appear in written accounts of practice, such as 'good practice' guidance. It is also sometimes referred to as 'craft knowledge'. It contrasts with the emphasis in formal knowledge on utilizing rational cognition as a basis for decision-making and action, instead emphasizing intuitive, 'gut instinct' responses. Though developed in practice scenarios, practice wisdom also incorporates the knowledge which practitioners possess by virtue of their own life experiences, thus arguably enhancing the breadth of practice wisdom.

Pointed criticisms have been levelled against practice wisdom, particularly the role of experiential knowledge. After all, if practitioners privilege personal experience, then a pertinent question would be 'what is the point of practitioners?' – that is, it is their knowledge over and above personal knowledge which differentiates social workers from their clients or others in society and thus legitimates and mandates their capacity to make decisions regarding other people's lives. More generally, there are questions about how, and on what basis, such knowledge can be differentiated from widely held 'common-sense' perspectives. It can also be difficult to promote consistent practice where practitioners draw upon differing knowledge which reflects their different life experiences. Variable practice, determined by individual preferences – or bias – may result. The disproportionate number of black service users in institutional mental health care is a good example. The personal aspect of tacit knowledge is therefore equated with subjective personal opinion or prejudice, rather than a validated component of the professional knowledge base. The contrary perspective is that it is not possible for practitioners to disregard personal experiences, and that this experience and reflection represents a valuable source of knowledge.

Exercise

Specify one defining characteristic, strength and limitation of formal and informal varieties of knowledge.

These controversies can usefully be explored further by reference to the 'art versus science' debate in social work. Arguably, the position that one takes regarding the nature and utility of these different 'varieties' of knowledge reflect positions taken in this related debate, which reflects the distinction between a broadly positivist paradigmatic position, in which knowledge is technical-rational in nature, and a broadly interpretive perspective, according to which knowledge is practical-moral.

Social work as 'art'

Within social work, the notion that art is a useful metaphor for understanding the nature of practice is enduring. Here, there is emphasis on the importance of the relationship between worker and client and the creative, inter-subjective process that they engage in. Key to understanding the attraction of this perspective is its emphasis on the creative interaction between worker and service user as a necessary pre-requisite for meaningful practice. This process is characterized as story telling, the basis for the co-construction of narratives. The ability of the client to partake in this encounter requires of the practitioner a process of artistic engagement or enabling which is itself creative.

Intuition is central to social work as 'art' and, according to Hugh England's influential account, represents a form of uncommonly developed common sense which can be counter posed with 'detached scrutiny' (1986: 28). Those who possess this capacity demonstrate unusual levels of empathetic understanding. As a corollary, abstract or theoretical knowledge is accorded secondary status compared to experiential skills. Instead, creativity is privileged and acknowledged as often intuitive, drawing upon internalized skills and capacities which may be difficult to articulate but which have meaningful impact in practice. This reflects an emphasis on the value of 'self', or what the practitioner brings to the interactional encounter. Creativity is privileged as a basis for the holistic synthesis of all of the component elements of a particular situation. Holism entails attention to all aspects of an individual's circumstances and functioning, both past and present, rather than to discrete elements of it, which contrasts with the emphasis on categories and classifications, inferences and variables which characterize more 'scientific' approaches to practice. Artistic practice entails a type of journey which the practitioner and service user undertake together, enabling practitioners to have some understanding of their client's distress and therefore to assist in their recovery. Formal knowledge is secondary to creative interpretation. Workers create solutions through their interpretations, rather than applying ready made, off the shelf answers to problems.

Practice as interpretation has been influential in social work, but has also attracted pointed criticism. Sheppard highlights 'an avoidance of precision...in favour of the use of metaphor' (2006: 170). How outcomes are actually achieved is 'shrouded in mystery' (ibid.). This makes it difficult for 'artistic' endeavour to be assessed – indeed, by definition, it is much more amenable to aesthetic judgement than to the rigours of evaluation. This in turn means that attempts to investigate and articulate what it is about social work which has effect – that is 'what works for whom and why' – are hampered, with implications for the credibility and legitimacy of agencies. As this is the major contemporary challenge for the profession, critics regard continued advocacy of such perspectives as distracting and counterproductive.

According to critics, then, artistic practice misrepresents what social work 'is', downgrading its social order role. It risks turning social work into a cosy personalized service such as counselling, rather than recognizing the fundamental significance of the state in determining the role, scope and mandate of social work. None of this is to deny that social work does, to some extent, entail the co-construction of meaning, or that intuition has an important function in the genesis of knowledge and understanding. However, like all perspectives, in its extreme version, it invites critique.

There are clear links between this 'artistic' notion of practice and the interpretivist position within social science. Both place great stress on meaning and interaction as the basis for understanding and action, and are thus subjectivist in orientation. As such, these are generally regarded as at odds with the objectivist stance which those who regard social work 'as science' tend to advocate.

Social work as science

To reiterate, science represents a means of generating knowledge according to a particular method, entailing the generation and testing of theories in the form of hypotheses. The production of knowledge fills gaps and reduces uncertainty, and so the potential utility of science to social work – a profession arguably defined by its relationship to uncertainty (Fook 2007) – is evident. Kirk and Reid refer to the lack of a distinctive scientific knowledge base as social work's 'Achilles heel' (2002: 6), particularly with regard to its status as a profession. It is 'mastery' of such knowledge, and the ability to apply it which defines professionalism. Enduring disputes regarding the status of social work as a profession suggest that the nature of the relationship between knowledge, science and practice in social work is problematic. This is because 'the "soft" nature of social work knowledge impedes cumulative knowledge building efforts' (ibid.: 25).

Whereas social work as 'art' entails autonomous, individualized, relationship based creativity, social work 'as' science entails the pre-defined proscriptive application of knowledge-based intervention in accordance with systems and processes which emphasize consistency. In such circumstances, some feel, the centrality of the relationship between service user and worker is devalued, and in the process the professional endeavour takes on a wholly different character. The ability of the practitioner and client to co-construct meaning on the basis of empathy and understanding is inhibited by an emphasis on compliance with pre-proscribed intervention programmes, form filling and tick boxes. None of these are professional tasks, properly understood, and so lay the ground for a process of de-skilling in which unqualified staff increasingly undertake roles and responsibilities which previously were firmly within the province of the professional practitioner. This, arguably, is exactly what has happened to the probation service since its de-coupling from social work in the late 1990s. It is science, rather than 'art', which undermines professionalism.

In essence, 'scientific' social work entails a deductive approach to knowledge use. There are links between deductivism and a 'technical instrumental' approach to the relationship between theory and practice, as well as notions that practice can and should be based on formal knowledge. Proponents of a scientific approach are unconvinced by arguments that natural science methods don't translate to social work. They claim that emphasis on social work as 'craft' has not served the profession or its users well. The claim is that via the application of scientific methods, social work would produce more reliable knowledge and thus enhance its effectiveness and legitimacy.

Sometimes, links are drawn between the rise of technicality and associated decline in indeterminacy, and managerialism (Howe 1991). Though managerial processes permeate all bureaucratic organizations, their recent extension tends to be associated with demands that the public sector demonstrate greater efficiency and effectiveness, a credo itself associated with the rise to prominence of a 'new right' political philosophy from the late 1970s onwards. Managerialism is seen as establishing the basis for restraints on practitioner discretion. Notions of competence place emphasis on compliance with policy and procedure. Some regard this as a process of de-professionalization, as autonomy is regarded as a defining trait of professionalism.

There is an evident lack of consensus, then, that the resolution of the social problems in which social work is mandated to intervene is best achieved via a knowledge as opposed to skills-based strategy. It has also been suggested that social work is neither art nor science. The distinction is artificial, useful for heuristic purposes but bearing little relationship to the realities of knowledge production or knowledge use in social work. Art and science represent two points on a continuum, with practice a hybrid amalgamation located somewhere towards the mid point. McLaughlin sees practice as 'both an art and science inextricably entwined in the personal and political' (2007: 79). The question still arises however: towards which pole should social work aspire if it is to address contemporary challenges adequately? We will explore these issues by reference to the links between paradigmatic positions and social work practice.

Exercise

Do you regard social work practice as closer to 'art' or 'science'? Justify your position.

Paradigms and practice

Here we outline what social work practice informed by the ideas and concepts associated with each of the paradigmatic perspectives we have discussed in the preceding chapters would entail. We highlight the distinguishing characteristics of particular positions and outline their strengths and limitations. We also highlight points of convergence which challenge the assumptions of the incommensurability thesis and therefore potentially represent the basis for some degree of disciplinary rapprochement.

Positivism and empirical practice

The empirical practice movement, or evidence-based practice, is based upon broadly positivist principles. The 'hierarchy of knowledge' is privileged, in which randomized control trials and systematic reviews are regarded as producing the most valid and reliable knowledge for practice. 'Scientific' principles and methods are applied so that evidence of effectiveness explicitly and directly contributes to decision-making and action. There is also a separate 'strand' concerned with ensuring that the focus is not just on pre-existing knowledge, but that practitioners are also equipped to develop 'new' knowledge.

Practice might be enhanced by a fuller engagement with science in two principal ways; either by the direct application of scientific method in practice, or by applying findings from scientific study to practice. The first of these relates to the concern that practitioners should be able to produce 'new' knowledge. Practitioners would utilize the principles and methods underpinning scientific research directly in their practice. This approach – the scientific practitioner model – entails the 'systematic gathering of information, careful study of individual clients, and decision-making about intervention based on the analysis of case data.' (Kirk and Reid 2002: 21). This is not necessarily far removed from the nature of social work practice in many environments, the difference being in the rigorousness with which the process and method are followed. Practitioners develop knowledge 'in action', rather than necessarily only applying 'off the shelf' knowledge prepared 'in advance'. The latter option has come to be known as evidence-based practice, or the empirical practice movement. Here, the results of empirical research studies, based on the explicit application of scientific research methods, are used to guide the development and intervention strategies which are then applied by practitioners, thus arguably better ensuring that practice is based upon more solid knowledge foundations than would otherwise be the case.

One means via which 'empirical' practitioners might 'make' knowledge is via the single system design (Kazi 1998), described by Kirk and Reid as the 'hallmark methodology' (2002: 93) of scientific practice. Its scientism is reflected in requirements that the nature of the problem to be addressed is outlined in a manner which is specific and observable, with data regarding the frequency or severity of this issue collected as a base line against which any change as a result of intervention can be compared. This enables problems to be tracked over time and inferences made about the possible effect of social work intervention in generating change. Note the reference here to 'inference'. There is no necessary assumption that data are direct representations of reality. In this respect, empiricism has links with realism. Translating such data into knowledge for practice is not necessarily as complicated as might be assumed. According to Sheldon and Macdonald, it requires 'the transparent reviewing of problems and their origins with clients, plus...discussion regarding what research of good quality has to say about what has been tried in cases such as theirs and to what effect' (2009: 79). This is not 'rocket science' (ibid.). Indeed, arguably there is disjuncture between the representation and the reality of scientific practice. Whether, in the UK at least, there are actually any examples of advocates of pure empiricism in social work is debatable. Rather, there are those who regard science, with all of its limitations, as preferable to relativism.

Practice guidelines, which combine research findings, systematic reviews and expert viewpoints are associated with evidence-based practice. These differ from more traditional 'good practice guidance' as these tend to be based principally on practice wisdom. They are intended as synthesizing overviews of the best available knowledge, and thus practitioners are not required to undertake research or engage in the lengthy process of reading research and assessing its validity and generalizability.

This model of the practitioner as clinical scientist, whereby scientific methods are applied in practice, new knowledge is generated according to similar principles and evidence of effectiveness informs intervention has provoked much debate (Webb 2001). Partly this is because of close links with cognitive behavioural approaches to practice. This prompts concerns that an emphasis on individualized 'cognitions' downplays the importance of past experience and social circumstances in causation, which some see as unethical or oppressive. Sheldon and Macdonald's position is clear, however: 'The results of systematic reviews and experiments show that...cognitive behavioural approaches never come second to anything' (2009: 64). Arguably, however, 'scientific social work' is far removed from custom and practice in agencies and therefore has struggled to realize its potential, remaining, for better or worse, a relatively marginal approach to practice (Sheldon et al. 2004).

There are also methodological limitations associated with empiricism as a means of producing knowledge of significance to practice. Attention focuses on the testing of hypotheses about the effect of intervention, rather than establishing how such intervention might actually work ('why what works works in this case'). 'Outcomes' are prioritized rather than 'processes'. As such 'empirical practice approaches are limited in addressing the full complexities of social work practice' (Kazi 2003: 16).

Interpretivism

In practice scenarios, the fit between interpretive assumptions and method is exemplified by those approaches to practice which stress the potential for reflection as a means for practitioners to better ensure that their practice is both ethical and effective. Key here is the work of Schon (1983) which represents a significant exposition of the necessity for, and benefits of, tacit knowledge. Contrary to the view that practice is best seen as entailing the application of pre-existing knowledge, Schon argues that theory, or knowledge utilized in practice, is only meaningfully articulated through action. This is because much of the reality of practice is far removed from how it is theorized. Indeed, because of this mismatch, practitioners must adapt generalized theory to the concerns of the individualized client or situation. This adaptability should in itself be seen as a central component of what it is to 'be' a practitioner, and it is around the notion of reflective practice that this idea has developed. Because of the unpredictability of the situations which social workers operate within, it is not possible to develop pre-proscribed responses, the aim of empirical approaches. The creative capacities of the practitioner are therefore called upon to circumvent the limitations of formal knowledge. Each situation therefore has its own unique character, as determined by the interaction between formal theory, experiential knowledge, intuitive responses and the particular characteristics of the 'case' in question.

Reflective practice takes issue, then, with 'top down' models of technical rationalism, in which practitioners apply ready-made knowledge in a formulaic manner in proscribed and circumscribed situations. Instead, tacit knowledge plays a much more significant role, and necessarily so, because the problems which practitioners must deal with are of a different nature to those which knowledge generated 'on high'. This context – the 'swampy lowlands' of practice – is such that practitioners must modify or interpret existing knowledge to make it useful for their immediate purposes. The assumption is that practitioners need, generate and use different forms of knowledge than that which is required by managers and policy-makers, but as it is managers and policy-makers who are influential in setting the agenda for knowledge production, practitioners have little option but to rely upon informal varieties. This also tallies with an interpretivist worldview, in that there is a divide between the managerial fixation on formal knowledge produced by positivist means which is assumed to correspond with 'reality', and the awareness held by practitioners that the problems with which they deal and the solutions which emerge are subjectively constructed rather than objectively determined.

Reflective practice specifies what practitioners do as entailing a combination of application, and reflection upon, knowledge. The first of these is referred to as 'knowing in action', utilizing intuition. Tasks are undertaken seemingly without the conscious recall and application of knowledge. There is also some degree of 'reflection in action' when 'the usual ways of doing things' are disrupted by novel circumstances, and so practitioners ask questions about the utility of their routine ways of acting and develop new approaches to resolving the difficulties with which they are faced. Subsequently, they may engage in retrospective reflection on their actions with a view to integrating the components of successful action into their existing knowledge base, a process referred to as 'reflection on action'.

This model places great emphasis on the capacity and value of practitioners utilizing their tacit, experiential knowledge ('know how') creatively. Accordingly, it downplays the value of more formal, technical-rational types of knowledge ('know that'). The ability to access intuitively and apply formal knowledge is assumed to develop with experience, with a related and notable decline in reliance on procedural guidance over time as practitioners proceed from 'novice' to 'expert' status. Accordingly, aspects of the role which were once fraught with potential difficulty actually become mundane and routine, in that they can be dealt with without recourse to extant knowledge and instead through intuitive knowledge. Reflection 'on' action enables practitioners to bring to the fore this tacit and experiential knowledge. It is important, however, not to disregard the extent to which such intuitive knowing may be based upon an underpinning bedrock of formal knowledge – that is, the two are complementary rather than competing.

From reflection to reflexivity

There have been efforts to broaden the focus of reflection via the integration of theoretical perspectives drawn from post-modernism and post-structuralism, as well as critical theory. Crucially, this involves acknowledgement of the intrinsic nature of subjectivity, and the development of strategies to enable participants to assess the role that contextual social, political and ethical factors play in the social work process and to use these as a basis for the development of effective solutions. Thus the notion of reflection has expanded into the wider notion of reflexivity, the key distinction being between the former's focus on internal self awareness and the latter's emphasis on ensuring that the role that external, contextual factors play in informing individual subjectivity is specified.

Reflexivity

Reflexive practice can be seen as a validation of aspects of Schon's work, but also as a critique, which seeks to take forward the notion of reflection by expanding is parameters. It is acknowledged that empirical practice has a role to play in contemporary social work, but also limits and disadvantages, not least its relative neglect of the processes entailed in practice. This contrasts with the emphasis which practitioners themselves place on trying to ensure that their judgements and decision-making are accurate and just by thinking seriously about what they do and why they do it. Reflective practice is regarded as perhaps the major forum via which practitioners can 'make meaning'. This is especially significant in relation to decisions regarding how to act, as in social work these are not straightforward, because they reflect the inherent complexity and ambiguity of the human subjects and situations with which workers are involved. As such, there are many circumstances in which formal knowledge is insufficient.

In theory, empirical practice represents a means of ensuring that necessary decisions are based on logic and rationality rather than mere opinion, bias or prejudice, therefore minimizing error, and enhancing quality and effectiveness. Perhaps counter-intuitively, however, such initiatives can contribute to a climate in which error is more rather than less likely. This is because practitioners may become over reliant upon formalized knowledge, neglecting skills required to make judgements and decisions where existing knowledge is not relevant or available, via skills such as 'reflection in action'. Despite the efforts of science, much of social work remains uncertain. The nature of knowledge is such that answers to all of the questions that need to be answered are not possible. This is because many of the decisions and actions which social workers need to make are moral or ethical rather than being of a nature which is amenable to resolution via scientific method.

So, although often social workers will draw upon formal types of knowledge, equally, they are required to make judgements between competing knowledge claims, some of which arise because the accounts of events which they have are either inaccurate or untrue. There are commonplace scenarios in practice where 'evidence' about how best to respond is limited, inconclusive or contested. Situations are complex, ambiguity is evident and decisions which need to be made are not technical or instrumental but ethical or moral. You will recall from Chapter 1 that such issues are metaphysical and beyond the bounds of science. In social work, practitioners are less likely to be dealing with hard and fast facts, accurate representations of uncontested reality, but instead conflicting versions of events, linguistically constructed according to the particular standpoints and worldviews of the respective participants. Choosing between accounts ultimately has to be a subjective process and is an unavoidable aspect of practice. Practitioners therefore engage in 'making knowledge' through their subjective judgements and the actions which follow. Thus, it is not feasible to portray decisions and actions by practitioners as being solely or ideally based upon an objective knowledge base derived from the application of the philosophy and methods of empirical science.

This perspective is supported by work in the sociology of science which demonstrates disjuncture between the rhetoric and reality of scientific research. Internally, science is riven by contention, with the knowledge bases of particular specialisms much less robust than is ordinarily assumed, and arrived at via processes which are as mundane and everyday as is the case in 'soft' disciplines. The essential role that subjectivity plays in scientific processes is manifest. If, even in science, pure objectivism is tempered by evident subjectivism, then the standard positivist critique of interpretivism is weakened. This prompts Taylor and White to emphasize Latour's (1999) notion of 'sturdy relativism', whereby knowledge claims are recognized as contested but nevertheless adequate. It is notable that 'sturdy relativism' is also known as 'realistic realism', suggesting that differences are not as stark as sometimes portrayed.

The suggestion, then, is that it is right and proper that knowledge be recognized as multiple and contingent, but that this in itself does not mean that knowledge cannot be used selectively in accordance with immediate practical requirements according to criteria of relevance, adequacy and utility. Decision-making by practitioners should therefore include careful appraisal of options and associated outcomes within a wider context in which 'everyday critical practices' are developed to ensure that there is congruence between overall purpose and situated decision-making. This reflexivity represents more than some ill-defined reflection. It is a means of bringing professional assumptions, or tacit knowledge, to the fore via critical analysis which makes explicit the links between practice, professional constructions and interpretations, and the wider social and political context.

Neither empirical practice nor reflective practice is sufficient as the basis for social work meeting the challenges it faces, and 'reflexive practice' represents an alternative option. Reflexivity refers to the collective disciplinary and individual practitioner's obligation to 'subject their own knowledge claims and practices to analysis' (Taylor and White 2000: 198). Whereas reflection is practice orientated, concerned with paying due attention to how practitioners apply theory to practice, reflexivity is more alert to the impact of taken for granted assumptions which underpin and legitimize knowledge and action for practice. Indeed, it is more willing to problematize the whole professional endeavour, rather than limiting its focus to what can be improved within the nature of the interaction between worker and service user. The intersection between knowledge and power in the constitution of professional roles and identities, and the tendency for certain perspectives (or 'voices') to be privileged, and others subjugated, are key in this process. The contingent and constructed – rather than absolute or certain – nature of knowledge is emphasized. Practice is defined by its relationship to the ubiquity of uncertainty. This is clearly at odds with the assumptions underpinning the drive for practice to be knowledge, or evidence, based, which conversely are concerned with the minimization of the uncertainty which here is seen as intrinsic.

Reflexive practice, then, asks that practitioners be both reflective about their work, but also integrate an understanding that the nature of their role and tasks are contextually and contingently constructed, rather than being actual reflections of reality. In meaningful terms, this asks that practitioners do their jobs in an awareness that the knowledge claims that they make in the process – this person is 'this sort' of person, the best way to deal with this issue is by way of this intervention – are not 'facts' but attempts to make meaning. This is well and good, but according to critics a separate challenge from the urgent need to counter the criticisms regarding social work's ability to effectively identify and manage risk and vulnerability and so bolster the standing of the profession.

Critical reflection

As we have seen, the key purpose of critical approaches to practice is to contribute to the empowerment or emancipation of oppressed groups and individuals in society. The assumption is that 'power operates through ways of knowing' (Everitt et al. 1992: 135). Key influences include feminist thinking, Marxism, and anti-oppressive theory. Generally, such perspectives are critical of individualizing approaches which downplay the significance of wider structural factors. Practice which is informed by such perspectives may be concerned with addressing material hardship, empowerment, consciousness raising, and with challenging institutionalized discrimination. It is debatable whether the current context positively enables these forms of practice. How professionals might respond therefore becomes an issue. This is where critical reflection may have potential (Fook 2002). It offers an alternative take on how we understand social work and how social work should respond to the challenges it faces.

Practitioners are seen as facing very particular challenges. These include how they adapt to changing expectations and responsibilities, and the issues these raise for value driven practice. The pervasiveness of concerns about risk and uncertainty arguably impinge upon holistic conceptualizations of role and task, hinder constructive practice, promote defensive practice, and perpetuate unrealistic expectations. Practitioners are left feeling powerless and confused regarding their role. The suggestion is that this reflects the dominance of a technical-rational model of professional practice, at the expense of a moral one, leading to value conflicts for practitioners.

Organizations respond in particular ways to concerns about uncertainty. It is assumed that if practitioner discretion can be minimized, then so can risk. Bureaucratic processes and procedures come to the fore, and there is a tendency to focus on specific components of practice and their relationship to outcomes rather than a more holistic, process orientated approach. This is associated with a concern with justifying organizational legitimacy through numbers – quantity rather than quality. Risk aversion is rife and practitioners become disillusioned and disempowered. Critical reflection aims to rectify this situation by exploring the fit between knowledge and expectations, thus facilitating the 'making' and 're-making' of knowledge appropriate to practice. It aims to enable practitioners to re-think their own assumptions about practice and therefore do things differently.

Though related to reflective practice and reflexivity, critical reflection is different from both. This reflects its principal concern with the relationship between the individual and society, and the capacity for individuals to change this if the assumptions underpinning how situations and behaviour are understood are uncovered. The aim is 'to unsettle the major assumptions on which ... practice is based, making connections between assumptions and beliefs about the social world'

(Fook and Gardner 2007: 15). Such assumptions will often have a basis in paradigmatic positions which are taken for granted and reflect dominant social mores. Awareness of their influence will open up opportunities to choose potentially new ways of practising. Cumulatively, then, critical reflection represents a process of highlighting and challenging assumptions to bring about changes in practice and thus outcomes.

There are evident links with reflective practice and reflexivity. There is a shared commitment to the value of tacit knowledge such that 'bottom up', inductively produced knowledge is accorded equal, if not greater, status with 'top down', deductively produced knowledge. As a corollary, practitioner intuition and 'artistry' are acknowledged as significant within professional practice, especially via the adaptation of existing knowledge and skills, or the generation of new knowledge, within novel contexts, and regarded as essential if practitioners are to be able to adapt to changing circumstances. Each is concerned with ensuring that practitioners are alert to the role that internal and external contextual factors bring to bear on their work. Subjectivity is significant – it informs and mediates the ways in which they focus on, interpret and use particular knowledge claims. As such, 'critical reflection becomes a way of researching the knowledge inherent in our practice, and connecting this knowledge (and ourselves) with our broader social contexts' (ibid.: 30). This is only possible if the connections between individual and social are clearly explicated. It involves re-emphasizing the links between the personal and the professional in social work practice, including the role that emotions play in interaction.

There are links between critical reflection and both critical theory and post-modernism. There is stress on the political nature of the relationship between the individual and society and the role that power plays in constituting the nature of this relationship – primary concerns of critical theory. Equally, social arrangements are experienced at an individual level and vary accordingly. Understanding of the effects of macro level wider social arrangements is integrated with the micro level situated perceptions of the individuals concerned – a post-modern perspective. Critical theory is seen as a necessary accompaniment to post-modern thinking because although the latter is useful for highlighting the need for alternatives to existing arrangements, it is less fruitful in specifying what form these might take. This is limiting where objectives are concerned with fairness, equity and social justice. Revealing knowledge as interpretation challenges dominant assumptions and provides space for alternative perspectives to have influence. Critical theory provides a framework for action, an orientation towards change.

The assumption in this approach, then, is not that agreement will necessarily be reached between worker and service user, but that different perspectives co-exist. Key practice techniques include, for example, the use of critical incident analysis and specific emphasis on creative and artistic methods. Approaches to interviewing are less adversarial and more participative, with 'more reflexive questions, to allow for multiple understandings or to include marginal perspectives' (ibid.: 177). Questions are used which seek to socially contextualize the individual's decision-making and action. Rather than seeking quick resolution via brief intervention, the process may become slower as practitioners become 'more inclined to explore complexity...sitting with uncertainty, waiting for individual clients to be ready to make decisions' (ibid.: 183). Links are also identified with other approaches to practice which share a basic orientation, around values and change. Nigel Parton (1998, 2000) in particular has been influential in seeking to delineate the implications for practice of working in conditions of complexity, uncertainty and ambiguity, making links with solution focused and narrative approaches, which are also informed by post-modern and critical theory and so fit well with this approach.

Numerous benefits are claimed for critical reflection. These include enabling practitioners to look at their work from different perspectives based on an understanding of the role that assumptions and values play in decisions and actions. This helps ensure that these are not neglected in deciding how to act. It is also recognized that practice cannot be neutral in its ethos, intent or effects, which should be to do with social justice for service users. Accordingly, there is emphasis on the interaction between the individual and the broader social context, rather than reliance on individualized models of explanation. It also claims to equip practitioners to tolerate inherent risk by emphasizing the ubiquity of uncertainty. Significance is attached to both process and outcomes, and as part of this, the valuable role played by subjectivity, intuition and tacit experiential knowledge, which are central to professional identity and thus esteem, is re-stated.

Critical reflection's post-modern and critical affiliations render it vulnerable to the standard accusations of relativism and bias which tend to be levelled against these paradigmatic positions. This is most evident with regard to the issue of the aims of practice which here are unequivocally seen as being concerned with the maximization of service user well-being. Some see this as misplaced – a perspective which is developed in the next section.

Realism and practice validity

The distinctiveness of realism as a framework for social work practice results from its emphasis on the need to be aware of the fact that interventions do not enter into a vacuum, but interact with other significant factors, not least the particular service user and the wider context within which they are located. It is this interaction which is central to how realists understand the relative success or failure of intervention, and which also alerts us to the reasons why practice which is effective with one service user may not 'work' with another.

The potential significance of critical realism for practice can be illuminated by reference to Howe's (1996) specification of 'surface' and 'depth' traits in social work. The relative priority accorded to either of these varies according to social and political context. Recent emphasis on relatively brief periods of intervention utilizing theories and models which emphasize the significance of 'here and now' factors can be contrasted with alternative approaches which attribute significance to 'depth level' issues in which wider experiences are attributed aetiological significance and are therefore deemed necessarily relevant in attempts to bring about change. Empirical models of practice arguably neglect concern with deeper issues to do with understanding persons and their situation, while interpretive approaches focus on these at the expense of an explicit concern with outcomes. Realism claims to offer potential to address the limitations of both by virtue of its concern with delineating the relationships between mechanisms, effects and contexts.

Realism's acknowledgement of the inherent difficulties in generalizing knowledge gained in one context to another, because of the different configuration of mechanism and context, problematizes the empiricist expectation that outcomes may be attributed to the application of a particular theory or model and therefore may be replicated by extrapolation. Instead, there is congruence with the emphasis in depth level approaches on more cautious and provisional proclamations on the nature of the relationship between cause, intervention and effect. However, and distinctively in comparison to interpretivism, despite this orientation, realism is not anti-empiricist. Instead, it seeks to integrate surface and depth.

This emphasis on the provisional nature of the knowledge claims is of a different nature to the emphasis within interpretivist perspectives on the ubiquity of uncertainty. Though both would avoid claims to generalizability, whereas interpretivists would actively seek to avoid making a judgement as to cause and effect, realists would seek to identify the tendencies at play in a particular case as a basis for understanding the nature of the issue at hand and the means of intervention which would follow. This might entail the refinement of knowledge via hypotheses generation and testing via falsification, undertaken within a framework in which knowledge claims are approached systematically and critically so as better to strengthen the status of knowledge (Sheppard 1995). Crucially, in terms of distinguishing realism from empiricism, these hypotheses are not limited to observable phenomena but also to unseen causal mechanisms which are hidden, at depth level.

In this framework, then, the value of a knowledge claim is tested by its value in enabling us to explain some issue which we are seeking to understand. Although empirical data are useful in this regard, the suggestion that these should be the only criteria via which the veracity of a knowledge claim is established is rejected. Nonetheless, there is a general affiliation within realism for formal rather than informal knowledge sources. Thus there are incompatibilities between realism and intuitive approaches to judgement and decision-making. There are, however, also links. The awareness that knowledge is partial and thus subject to revision means that practitioners need to guard against the assumption that their current position is definitive – that this person is high risk, for example. This is also acknowledged in reflexive practice. Instead, they should recognize that there are reciprocal interactions between professional judgements and decisions, mechanisms and contexts which are wider than their interactions with service users.

A distinctive realist approach to practice has been developed by Michael Sheppard (1995, 1998, 2001, 2003, 2006). Again, there is emphasis on social work as having 'durable and stable' 'depth' level traits which are manifest over and above any superficial, surface level changes in policy or practice which may occur. Realists therefore take issue with those who suggest that social work has no 'essence' but is instead contextually determined according to prevailing social and political influences (Cree 2002, Parton 1998). Despite evident change at surface level which some regard as challenging the basis and ethos of practice, nevertheless there is continuity at a depth level and so social work remains a stable enterprise.

Certain 'depth' characteristics are specified as defining the nature of social work (Philp 1979). These include the unique 'space' it fills at the interface between mainstream and marginal, where the interests of competing sections of society are mediated between, and whereby private interests become public concerns. The latter indicates affiliation to 'the state', whereby it is right, proper and possible to intervene in the lives of individuals in the interests of the collective, sometimes in the process violating other principles, such as self determination. The 'override criterion' tends to be one of potential harm or vulnerability. Next, objectivity and subjectivity interact. The objective status of social problems also accommodates a concern with the power of objective 'states' to determine and have constituting effects upon those to whom they are applied. This necessitates 'creating subjectivity (the person) out of objective states (the label)' (Sheppard 2006: 41). In practical terms, this means that social workers aim to 'paint a picture' of the service user's inherent humanity by placing individual functioning or behaviour within its social context. This objectivity allies social work with a consensus model of society. Finally, social work is an interactional endeavour, comprising three components: interaction between worker and client; an emphasis on understanding individual behaviour as occurring within a social context; and an overarching framework which entails a relationship between the individual and the state. Key is the meeting between social worker and service user, as it is through this medium that interactional potential is realized. This reflects an orientation towards the individual as a vehicle for achieving social ends. Additionally, the positioning of social work between mainstream and marginal contributes to an underlying humanitarianism which helps account for an abiding concern with the welfare of the individual. The interaction of these facets differentiates social work from other activities, professions and disciplines.

Certain implications flow from this understanding of social work. Central among these is the form that social work takes in practice. Understanding social work as a practice-based discipline implies that the knowledge which it draws upon should be consistent with the nature of the roles and tasks which practitioners undertake, and with the assumptions underpinning these. This has significance to the debate about the nature of the relationship between theory and practice, in that often particular methods are advocated irrespective of the practice scenario in which they are to be applied. Partisan advocates seek to generalize the strengths of their particular affiliation to apply to all situations and service users. This is a fraught enterprise, as there is no evidence that any one theory, method or worldview 'holds' across such diverse situations, and ample to suggest the opposite. In the face of such limitations, it is perhaps more sensible to limit ambitions by criteria of relevance and utility. Here the notion of the 'practice paradigm' is significant.

To reiterate, a paradigm equates to a distinctive worldview or perspective which provides a unifying framework for thought and action among those who share or subscribe to its principles. Knowledge which is useful for social workers, then, will be knowledge which accords with its underpinning assumptions. Where it does, knowledge is deemed to have 'practice validity', and it is practice validity which determines the parameters of disciplinary endeavour, differentiating social work from other, related disciplines, such as social care, counselling, or policing. Thus, knowledge in social work must not only satisfy the criteria of methodological rigour – validity, generalizability, coherence – which define 'epistemic validity' in the social sciences, but also the 'fundamental criterion' of relevance and utility in practice.

Sheppard suggests that social workers should be regarded as 'rule using analysts' and 'hypothesis generators and testers'. They use hypotheses to make sense of people and situations and revise these in light of new information in a process of constant hypotheses generation and testing. Practitioners' views are provisional, in line with realist principles, and as such always subject to potential overturning by the discovery of new knowledge or information. Indeed, this is a possibility which practitioners should actively aspire to bring about by testing the veracity of their knowledge and assumptions and the actions which follow from these. The intention is to ensure 'fit' between theory and practice.

In situations where the limits of knowledge are accepted, practitioners also need to be able to develop new knowledge. Thus analytic capabilities come to the fore, with hypotheses generation and testing representing a means of developing alternative means of making sense of a situation and deciding how to act. This process is 'retroductive', entailing both intuition and critical analysis. Pre-existing means of making sense are drawn upon intuitively unless and until they are no longer deemed sufficient to the task in hand, in which case analytic capabilities will be drawn upon. Retroduction, then, combines both inductive and deductive logics of enquiry and explanation, and both formal and informal (tacit) knowledge. Deduction is used to test hypotheses regarding what is occurring in a particular situation and induction to develop (or build) alternative theories. In practice, this will often mean that practitioners apply a particular theoretical framework or approach to making sense of and intervening with which they are already familiar. If it 'holds' – that is, it is of ongoing utility – it will in all likelihood set the parameters for the nature and scope of work throughout the period of involvement. Where it does not, that is, the practitioner believes that the connections between context, mechanism and outcomes which a particular theory posits are not correct in this case, an alternative theoretical perspective will be required. In some circumstances this will require an assessment of the utility of the existing theories which the practitioner has in his or her 'toolkit'. In others, it will entail the development of new theory or hypotheses.

The need for an approach to knowledge generation such as this relates to the discretionary gap left by the limits of scientific knowledge. Knowledge cannot provide all of the answers to all of the situations with which social workers need to deal. Even where there is significant evidence that a particular strategy has demonstrable efficacy is alleviating or addressing certain factors, it often will not work, and will not necessarily 'translate' into alternative scenarios where key characteristics and variables are likely to be of a different nature or status. You will recall that the need for such capacity is also acknowledged in reflective practice, reflexivity and critical reflection.

The model outlined here does not view social workers as either artists or scientists, but rather as engaged in processes of practical reasoning requiring the application of practical intelligence drawn from formal and informal knowledge, practice and life experience to complex, ambiguous situations. The suggestion that because knowledge may not be 'certain' then 'anything goes' is challenged by realism, which acknowledges the necessarily provisional nature of knowledge, but retains a commitment to providing the best possible understanding available at a particular juncture, as an 'orienting device' (Kirk and Reid 2002). Realism cannot promise certainty, but is premised on the belief that it is possible to know things with more certainty if certain principles adhere.

Exercise

Of the various approaches to making and using knowledge in practice, which do you find most convincing and why? What are the strengths and limitations of the perspective you prefer?

Rapprochement?

Perhaps unsurprisingly, it is those who are more sympathetic to interpretivist ideas who have been most vocal in their critique of realism (White 1997, 2001). For our purposes, however, it is enough to be aware that this debate is ongoing. What should also be apparent – and hopefully, we have demonstrated – is that despite the evident differences of ethos and method associated with alternative paradigmatic positions, certain concerns are shared.

Pure positivism, certainly of the type portrayed in critical caricature, is rare. Taylor and White (2001) acknowledge that debates between art and science may have generated more heat than light. Although they firmly advocate the merits of interpretive social science, they are sympathetic to a weak, or 'subtle' form of realism in which the contested nature of truth is to the fore, but the potential for science to limit, but not eliminate, uncertainty is acknowledged. Realists, although committed to an objectivist understanding of social work and its knowledge base, nevertheless acknowledge the constructed nature of the social work enterprise and the value of a critical stance towards the status quo (Stepney and Popple 2008). In particular, all parties assume that practitioners need to be able both to apply existing knowledge and develop new knowledge, and that this is central to efforts to improve the quality of practice and outcomes. 'Art' and 'science' are therefore arguably best seen as complementary rather than competing.

Practitioners, no doubt, find these debates distant from the practical endeavour which characterizes their day-to-day working lives. There does, however, appear to be scope for rapprochement between these varying positions, which might better equip social work to meet contemporary challenges. We turn our attention to this task in the conclusion.

7

The Agency: Shaping a Learning Organization

Ian Shaw

The scene for this book was sketched in Chapter 1 – a scene which drew on a framework of different sources of knowledge in social work and social care – organizations, service users, practitioners, researchers and the policy community. We have talked about each of these sources of knowledge in the subsequent chapters, leaving until now the first in the list – organizations. What we know, what we assume about what we know, and how our practice is influenced by what we know, are all influenced by the sources of our knowledge. In this chapter we focus primarily on the reality that all social workers – even self-employed social work consultants – are affected in their work by organizational knowledge.

We will develop ways in which practitioners can contribute to a learning culture in their practice and agency. While we are focusing on organizations, we will not be discussing how agencies are managed. Rather, the key learning point for this chapter is how practitioners can be effective members of organizations. In this sense, 'management' is seen as a cluster of knowledge, skills and values that all social workers need to gain and exercise. This idea of management as a practice skill is familiar to social workers in the phrase 'care management'. The questions this raises include:

- How can positive aspects of organizational culture be identified and embedded?
- If embedded, how can social workers contribute to sustaining good practice in an organization, so that it does not atrophy?
- What kinds of learning take place – and ought to take place – within social work agencies?

We will see that these questions are not only about knowledge and skills but also include value questions. While a diversity of approaches is part and parcel of good practice, they all to some degree involve value questions. A learning organization will, to a greater or lesser degree, be relatively egalitarian, and set questions of moral choices at the forefront of practice. Later in this chapter we will expand this point by illustrating how practitioner involvement in shaping a learning agency will involve goals and practices around evidence, understanding and justice. Before doing so, we will elaborate the part that *learning* plays in an organization. Evidence-based practice approaches are guided by the assumption that an agency will be transformed by having information on how well it is doing. Learning from information is rarely as simple as this. However, the assumption is helpful in that it illustrates how our views about how to improve practice in an agency are driven by an implicit theory of change – in this case, a theory that clear evidence about performance will produce change for the better.

Learning and social work organizations

Learning is 'essentially the way in which individuals develop meaning out of data they encounter' (Rogers and Williams, 2006: 77). Linking this to social work practice, one kind of learning is when we assess whether we have carried out our social work in accord with our goals. Within our present way of viewing our practice, have we done it better? A different kind of learning occurs when we do not simply ask if we have done something right, but rather, have we done the right thing. For example, we may have achieved our goals but were these the right goals to meet the needs of these service users?

This has sometimes been called the difference between single-loop learning and double-loop learning. 'Not just "were the prescribed procedures followed?" but also "is the thinking behind these procedures appropriate?"' (Rogers and Williams, 2006: 78).

These two options do not exhaust how learning takes place in organizations. There is also a question of how we learn to learn. This involves the process of critical reflection that we talked about in Chapter 6, and you can find a fuller account in that chapter. In this chapter we add a different example of how critical reflection – falsification – enables social workers to learn how to learn. The example is based on the work of the philosopher, Karl Popper. Popper was opposed to the older and generally discredited positivism of the early twentieth century. The assumption that positivism in social work is now more or less discredited and rarely espoused is not accepted by some social work writers. The American writer Bruce Thyer is an example of a committed positivist (e.g. Thyer, 1989), and an example of writers who believe it is alive and (dangerously) well are Everitt and Hardiker, 1996.

Popper told the story of how, early in his career, he visited the psychotherapist, Alfred Adler, famous for his work on the idea of the inferiority complex. Adler invited Popper to observe him in his consulting room, and later indicated that a person he had just seen exhibited the symptoms of an inferiority complex. Popper tells us that he asked Adler how he knew this to be the case. 'Because of my thousand fold experience', Adler apparently replied. The young Popper, too clever by half we may think, could not resist the retort, 'And now I suppose it is your thousand and one fold experience'!

Popper's concern was that Adler's way of explaining his practice was proceeding by searching for constant confirmatory instances. And that this approach led him down the path of promoting a theory that would ultimately be unfalsifiable. The risk is just as great in social work almost a hundred years later. The idea of a defence mechanism (e.g. projection, transference, or denial) may be helpful in therapeutic approaches to social work – but only so when we are careful to avoid the position where every kind of evidence serves to 'prove' our view. This can happen when, for example, a service user's resistance to the idea of exhibiting a defence mechanism is interpreted to be a sign of *resistance* (e.g. 'denial') and therefore to indicate the validity of the therapist's initial interpretation. The idea of 'false consciousness' in Marxist thinking is another example of a way of thinking that easily slips into being unfalsifiable, and in just the same way as the defence mechanism example – denial is seen as proof positive.

Concerns about 'false memory syndrome' in the field of child abuse provide a third example. They illustrate how difficult it can be to think clearly. The opposing claims that therapists have been subtly putting ideas into children's heads and that children have been enabled to surface lost memories about real abuse may continue to be disputed because of the difficulty of falsifying either claim. But learning how to learn requires practice skills that include a commitment to seeking to do so. Social workers could at least proceed by routinely asking themselves whether their practice tends to proceed by searching for confirming instances, and if they can specify the circumstances under which they would be prepared to reject a specific explanation or adherence to a particular practice model. (See Shaw 1996: 111–14 for a fuller plea for a falsifying approach.)

Learning organizations

But learning and learning how to learn are not simply individual tasks. They will always be at risk and hard to sustain unless the agency's organization culture and dynamics support such learning. But this is easier said than done. We can suggest some working rules for the kind of organization that will promote learning. For example, we have talked elsewhere in the book about the importance of aiming to make our mental models and assumptions explicit. Once again, this involves a process of reflection. We will introduce two further 'rules' about ways that practitioners can facilitate organizational learning that is sustainable.

First, think in a systemic way about how people, teams and service users interact with each other. For example, it will often be the case that our practice is guided not only by formal rules but also by informal rules. Informal rules are less likely to be explicit, but are those actions, judgements and recognitions that we accomplish spontaneously. We do not have to think about them prior to their 'performance' and we are often unaware of having learned to do them. They have become 'thinking as usual' knowledge. Social workers sometimes refer to 'common-sense knowledge' or 'practice wisdom' in this connection.

Hall gives an interesting example of this point in his ethnographic study of a hostel for homeless young people (Hall 2001). He describes how, in early interviews with staff at the hostel, he tended to get 'official', formal accounts of the work that went on. Central to these accounts was the place of arranging for each resident to have a 'key worker' to work individually with the young person, and make and review plans with the eventual aim of helping them to leave the accommodation. Yet he was increasingly struck from his field notes with how little time was actually spent in key working. It soon became obvious that staff spent far more time in everyday and informal contact with the residents. While this may appear 'obvious', he also realized that such everyday interaction was not mere 'background noise', but was central to the staff team's agenda.

> The daily schedule at the hostel; the rules of occupancy; the shopping, cooking and cleaning rotas for residents; all of these and many other

relatively minor arrangements...carried an ideological charge that had to do with establishing and encouraging certain attributes, standards and competences. (Hall 2001: 7)

Being both a participant and an observer – acting rather like an anthropologist – is one valuable way of understanding the importance of our own and our colleagues' informal, tacit and hence neglected organizational knowledge.

Second, understand and contribute to the part played by team and other forms of joint working. Organizational learning is always shared, joint learning, and calls for an appreciation of organizational dynamics. The first rule is insufficient. Indeed, if not adopted in a sensitive way, it could lead to an intellectual detachment from the work of the organization or agency – too much observation and not enough participation. But taken together they facilitate and promote new perspectives – looking at the organization from the bottom up rather than conventional ways of top down perspectives; awareness of informal rules; of conflict and bargaining; of unpredicted events; and of external influences. The idea that social workers can helpfully be seen as 'street level bureaucrats', discussed elsewhere in this book, is one example of such understanding.

Evidence, learning and justice

Our emphasis so far in this chapter has been on perspectives that promote creative understanding of the social worker's role and potential for organizational change. Translating this understanding into practice skills is not easy.

Taking in new information, developing meanings from that information, and using it to change behaviour can be surprisingly difficult, particularly when the information does not match with deeply implicit assumptions, mental models or habitual behaviour. (Rogers and Williams 2006: 92).

In this next part of the chapter we introduce examples of individual and collective practice skills that can change the culture of an organization. We base these skills on three related principles of good practice.

1. Social workers should practice in the light of the best *evidence* about what works well for service users.

2. This is one necessary basis for service users and carers to receive service that is fair, *just* and enabling.
3. Following from these two principles, service users, carers and the organizations in which they work are the better able to collaborate when they gain the capacity to learn about and *understand* both problems and ways in which they can be solved.

Evidence: practitioner enquiry

The example of developing organizational evidence that works well for service users is practitioner enquiry. McLeod has defined practitioner research as 'research carried out by practitioners for the purpose of advancing their own practice' (McLeod 1999: 8). We should add '...and/or that of their colleagues'. There have been several arguments in support of practitioner research in social work, two of the most frequently heard being the professional obligation to be self-evaluating, and the belief that research and practice draw on similar skills. McIvor aptly expressed these twin views when she says,

> The starting point...is the twofold belief that practitioners should be encouraged to engage in the evaluation of their own practice and that they possess many of the skills which are necessary to undertake the evaluative task. (McIvor 1995: 210)

The two examples of different projects in Box 7.1 illustrate what is typically involved. But solitary practitioner projects will not develop organizational learning unless ways are found to link them. Social work also requires the development of networks of practitioner research projects. This will prove demanding, but there is some encouraging precedent that suggests it may be feasible. For example, Knud Ramian, working in Denmark, has co-ordinated a substantial integrated programme of practitioner research on mental health rehabilitation, conducted through collaborative research networks (this information is taken from unpublished papers provided by Ramian). In this setting, he defines practitioner research as research carried out by practitioners who spend 80 per cent of their time on practice work. The research is done by practitioners in their agency, and focuses on problems in the daily life of the practitioner. Projects must be feasible and communicated to the practitioner community. A network involves 6–9 teams from rehabilitation units spread over the country. Each team includes two or three practitioners. A network

Box 7.1 Examples of Practitioner Enquiry

Example 1
The practitioner researcher engaged in the study was a support worker with people with learning difficulties and challenging behaviour. She had carried out the project for a postgraduate master's qualification in social work. She got interested in carrying out a master's degree through discussions at workshop sessions at the university. She was examining the effects of aggressive challenging behaviour on care staff in the learning disability services and the coping strategies staff use. She regarded the project as hers. It was a lone piece of work and the main setting in which the research took place was the local authority and two independent organizations – a housing agency and a university based voluntary agency. The location setting of the project was supported accommodation.

The project involved semi-structured interviews. She interviewed local authority support workers and workers from the other two organizations who provided support work. The main beneficiaries of the project were staff dealing with people with learning difficulties. The audiences for the project report were managers and staff of the particular Social Services Department. The project had not applied for formal ethical approval after it had been discussed in detail with the university tutor, who felt it was not necessary.

Example 2
A study of a community re-enablement scheme compared a traditional day hospital with a day centre. The main agency setting was in Social Services and the Health Service. The re-enablement 'team' owned the project and included centre staff, Day Hospital staff, community nurses, the client group within the team and the team itself. The local Health Group and Social Services funded the project. The main service user beneficiaries were older people living in the local authority. The audience for the project report consisted of the steering group for the Trust, which included the Director of Social Services, General Manager of the Local Health Group, Project Manager and consultants. It was a multiple data type, including a satisfaction survey (clients by post and interview) and a dependency scale. The Project Manager did not have to request Ethics Committee approval. The evaluation was carried out with the Day Centre Manager, her deputies and the nurse. An outside academic had an important input into the evaluation process.

[Both examples taken from a study of practitioner research (Shaw 2005)] shares a common research theme and works for approximately eighteen months. There have been more than twelve such networks hitherto, with 51 different teams, accounting for 110 participants. Each project is funded for the equivalent of two months' salary, with a contractual requirement that employers provide appropriate and defined working conditions for the participants. The programme as whole is partly held together through a 24-hour seminar every second month.

Practitioners should lobby their employers for the relatively modest financial resources needed to make this collective effort feasible.

Justice

Practitioner research is not only about best evidence. It also raises questions about the balance between practitioner and service user interests – and this is a justice question. Whereas in Chapter 3, the concern was with the extent to which service user voices are adequately represented in more general research practice, here the question is whether practitioner research should give primacy to service user and carer interests when agreeing a research agenda. For example, is it the case that 'insider' knowledge claims by service user and carer researchers, other things being equal, are always (or most of the time) better grounded and more trustworthy than 'outsider' knowledge claims?

We can illustrate the importance of this question from an interesting piece of research and writing in a paper by a black lesbian social work researcher, Valli Kanuha (Kanuha 2000). Kanuha struggled with the need for 'distance', aware that the intensity with which 'insider' researchers recognize and even identify with emotions can make it *harder* to discern patterns of emotion. She found her own self-reflections prevented her from focusing on the interview process.

> The need to separate my own experiences and subsequent analyses from those of study participants, with our natural connections yet distinctive roles as researcher-researched, was the most profound methodological process I had to learn as an insider researcher. (442)

Her efforts to create distance also proved counterproductive, preventing her from gaining rich descriptions of complex phenomena. Another conflict she encountered was in connection with having shared and taken for granted knowledge. She met vague statements that she did not probe or follow up.

> I thought, mistakenly or not, that I could somehow intuit what respondents meant by innuendoes about culturally specific behaviors, events, or analyses, or what I refer to as coded language. (442)

She set herself to counter these, so that when people said something like 'You know how white people can be sometimes', she would make a clarifying probe. She would vigorously pursue exceptions; and also sustain a kind of 'artificial officiousness' so that when she and her partner were invited to a meal with a study respondent and her partner, 'I was both troubled and honoured. I understood culturally why both my partner and I must go to the dinner, and all the methodological reasons why it was wholly inappropriate to do so' (443). She came to conclude that the insider 'represents one possible perspective' and that the insider 'is no longer just another native' (444).

Justice issues challenge at almost every point of social work practice. At a fairly modest level, agencies often routinely seek to learn if service users have been satisfied with the service they have received. However, as with practitioner research, this kind of exercise rarely has an impact on the culture of the organization. What can student social workers or practitioners do to challenge this? First, they can develop and plead for an approach that avoids individualism and maximizes the likelihood that users' views will be heard and acted upon. There are six ways in which good practice can be made more likely.

First, service users or their representatives should be *consulted* regarding how they wish their views to be canvassed.

Second, mechanisms must be in place to take up any *action arising* from service users' appraisals. Practitioner and management acceptance of client feedback will depend on believing that beneficial change is possible as a consequence. These mechanisms should include ways in which serious allegations against social workers are to be handled.

Third, routine satisfaction information needs to be enriched by more occasional, and *more thorough exercises*. These should be carried out by someone who is not in a position to invoke sanctions, real or imaginary, against service users who criticize services.

Fourth, satisfaction information is too often restricted to the collection of views regarding the delivery of services and perceived benefits. It should be widened to include efforts to learn people's views about a particular *problem*, and their opinions about the benefits and risks of introducing *service changes*. Focus groups can be used for this purpose.

Fifth, social workers should not rely on global ratings of service user satisfaction. Satisfaction must always be understood in the light of service users' *aspirations and expectations*. It will be helpful to distinguish between preferred (or ideal) expectations, and practical (or realistic) expectations. A general response saying 'satisfied' may mean any of the following:

- I've evaluated the service and I'm happy with it.
- I don't think I have the ability to evaluate but I do have confidence in the staff.
- The service was appalling but I don't like to criticize; after all they're doing their best.

Sixth, a word of caution. User satisfaction, without other evidence, should not normally be regarded as an indication of practice success. Rather than providing a guide to the success of the service in meeting either its own goals or those of the clients, such measures, without the infrastructure suggested above, relate primarily to the quality of the encounter between worker and client, not to its outcome.

Once these steps have been undertaken and agreed within the agency, teams can apply the framework to their own practice in the following way:

- Decide *how* the team will set about discovering the views of the relevant people (this may be in groups or individually; done by those with immediate case accountability or by someone from elsewhere in the agency or from outside the agency). Make notes of the strengths and limitations of the method.
- Work towards a number of *questions* team members would want to ask service users with whom they have worked (or are working).
- Think through what will be done with the *answers* that the social worker (or someone else in your agency or from outside) will receive.
- Consider how well this planned approach meets the good practice suggestions described above.
- Consider how far an agency should develop ways of addressing service user satisfaction that are the same across the agency or different for each service user group.

Understanding and learning

The most common image of doing practitioner research is of the practitioner as a scientific practitioner. It was for that reason we located the main discussion in the part of the chapter dealing with evidence. As we have seen, it is also relevant to embedding justice concerns in an agency. But even this does not exhaust the relevance of practitioner enquiry. McLeod, writing about counselling, complains that what is missing is 'knowledge-in-context' practitioner research, using methods of enquiry that are largely qualitative. This sets practitioner enquiry as a skill that promotes critical reflection and practice learning. It 'addresses the moral and ethical issues associated with the combination of researcher and practitioner roles, and with a process of enquiry into the experience of perhaps vulnerable or fragile informants... The findings represent subjective, personal knowing as well as objective, impersonal or "factual" knowledge' (McLeod 1999: 8, 9).

But more is needed if this is to become part of sustainable organizational knowledge. One practice method that promotes interactive learning is peer interviewing to foster critical reflective learning. The broad purpose of such interviews is to foster peer exploration of practice in contexts where the intention is to promote reflection on the dimensions of good and less good practice forms. The assumption is that most practitioners can, when asked, identify instances where their work has gone 'well' or 'not well', but that routine practice does not promote awareness of the assumptions, judgements and lesson-learning that are an implicit part of such identifications.

We have included a possible interview schedule that can be utilized for this purpose, although we stress that this should not be treated in a prescriptive manner, and there are necessary variations according to the agreed purpose of the interview. The interview will take somewhere between 30 and 75 minutes. It should be taped and wherever possible transcribed. The consequent debriefing is best undertaken either as a joint exercise, or by arranging for a trusted colleague with some knowledge of research interviewing and analysis to undertake a preliminary reflection on the transcript.

The peer dimension is central to this exercise. The task as a whole is relevant to developing social work skills relevant to innovation, change and expertise in organizations. Once again, it is important to recall that this is not about how best to manage, but about practice skills. An example from a UK children's service will illustrate how

Box 7.2 Reflective Peer Interviewing

Reflective Peer Interview Sample Schedule
I am going to ask you to talk about two recent examples of your own direct practice. One example will be about work that you think went well, and one will be about an example of your work in which you think you were practising less well. Please decide in your mind which examples you want to talk about, and also which one you prefer to talk about first.

1. Please briefly describe the work, especially telling me what went well/ less well.
2. How did you know you were doing this well/less well?
3. What was the evidence you actually used in this instance?
4. If we were able to talk to the people on the receiving end of your practice, do you think they would have held similar views? Would they have used similar or different criteria in judging whether the work had gone well or not?
5. Are you happy that your own yardsticks for judging whether or not you were practising well were the right ones in this instance?

Repeat the sequence of questions for the second piece of work. Then ask:

- Is there anything that these examples raise for you? For example, did they illustrate anything about the way you evaluate your own work?

expertise and innovation depend on practitioners as much as managers, and how such skills are often informal and unplanned. The example is from a children's services department introducing the Integrated Children's System (ICS) with an electronic record and range of exemplar records at its core. A focus group of practitioners, team leaders and managers have been discussing how far people have become expert in using the ICS. Box 7.3 gives a synopsis of this part of the conversation.

This example illustrates how practitioners sometimes acquire expertise during innovations that enable them to exercise, and suggest how others may exercise, discretion. In this case it appears that this discretion – which could be interpreted as rule-breaking – is accepted implicitly as a positive response by Colin, the manager.

A further way in which understanding and learning can be enhanced is through emerging ideas about Communities of Practice (CoP). These often may operate online through virtual communities. In

---

Box 7.3 Expertise in Children's Services

Alison (a social worker) went on to mention some specific examples of how her expertise might be called upon. She said that she tries to encourage practitioners to think creatively when making use of ICS forms. She said that social workers often feel compelled to fill in every part of the form and said that sometimes she advises social workers to leave some parts blank if the box is not relevant. She said that she often tries to encourage social workers to have the confidence to make decisions about which sections to leave blank.

Colin (a manager) went on to argue that social workers themselves can become experts. He said that during the process of rollout into teams...the role of social workers who have experience of the system is critical. He explained how these practitioners can use their experience and knowledge to provide support to workers in other teams in a way that managers cannot. He argued that social workers have credibility when they impart knowledge to other social workers that managers do not. He said that social workers are often more likely to take seriously advice from other social workers with direct experience of using the system, rather than from managers who might be seen as having a more detached relationship to ICS.

---

many ways CoPs are very much like informal networks, and so extend beyond a single organization or agency. Their distinctive nature lies in when such communities develop – or are initiated – with a focus on a particular domain of knowledge and the purpose of gaining knowledge and expertise through their continuing interaction. It is difficult to recall that the general access to email is still much less than twenty years old at the time of writing. The impact of the advent of email, in facilitating international networking in the social work community is hard to reimagine.

Proponents of virtual CoPs believe that such communities 'can be an effective mechanism for balancing the shortage of available evidence and the development of actionable knowledge or practice' (Cook-Craig and Sabah 2009: 727). They proceed to say that they:

> [P]rovide a new, geographically unbounded opportunity to create, verify, store and diffuse knowledge in the profession...(they) also offer an opportunity for practitioners to develop weak ties...(and) gain new knowledge and ways of practice *across* organizations and disciplines. (p. 728)

Without wishing to discourage practitioner engagement with CoP opportunities, several cautions need to be borne in mind. LaMendola et al. (2009) report a small but careful research study from which they conclude – in line with other studies – that such networks are likely to 'function regardless of media, meaning that such communities can be supported by, but are not necessarily an effect of, communication technology employment itself' (p. 721). Their results also indicated that practitioners viewed online contact as a supplement to face-to-face contact, and that the most beneficial activities were those that were face-to-face. This conclusion echoes the results of a study, also in Scotland, of a network of social workers engaged in practitioner research, and supported by staff from a university social work programme through a mix of face-to-face and email contacts (Lunt, Shaw and Mitchell 2009).

While virtual CoPs are unlikely to offer a panacea, staying alert to existing and emerging communities could allow social workers – to echo Cook-Craig and Sabah (2009) – to create, assess, store and diffuse knowledge in the profession, and offer an opportunity for practitioners to develop otherwise weak ties through gaining new knowledge and ways of practice *across* organizations and disciplines. Take, for example, the huge amount of digitization that is happening through libraries and elsewhere. This offers opportunities to social workers to press for archiving of recent and earlier parts of the profession's heritage (cf. Daly and Ballantyne 2009).

During this chapter we have reviewed how practitioners can be effective members of organizations. This involved us reflecting on the learning process. We referred to single-loop learning and double-loop learning, and how we learn to learn. We gave an example of how critical reflection through falsification enables social workers to learn how to learn.

We suggested some working rules for the kind of organization that will promote learning, in particular that we should think in a systemic way about how people, teams and service users interact with each other, and understand and contribute to the part played by team and other forms of joint working.

In the second part of the chapter we introduced examples of individual and collective practice skills that can change the culture of an organization. We based these skills on three principles of good practice. Social workers should practice in the light of the best *evidence* about what works well for service users so that service users and carers receive service that is fair, *just* and enabling, and also that they, service users, carers and the organizations in which they work gain the capacity to learn about and *understand* both problems and ways in which they can be solved. We will return to these three principles of evidence, understanding and justice in Chapter 8.

8

Evaluating in Practice

Ian Shaw

A subterranean distinction has rumbled along beneath the chapters of this book. Sometimes the argument has been organized with the general aim of showing how substantive knowledge from different kinds of research and enquiry can make for good social work practice. On other occasions the authors have focused more on how different ways of disciplined thinking and enquiry constitute indispensable elements of practice.

The distinction is neither accidental nor lacking consequence. Bill Reid, the inventor of task-centred intervention, expressed it as follows:

> Historically, the influence of science on direct social work practice has taken two forms. One is the use of the scientific method to shape practice activities, for example, gathering evidence and forming hypotheses about a client's problem. The other form is the provision of scientific knowledge about human beings, their problems and ways of resolving them. (Reid 1998: 3)

The example Reid gives of how ways of disciplined thinking and enquiry constitute indispensable elements of practice is 'gathering evidence and forming hypotheses about a client's problem'. The authors have referred to this approach previously. It is one of the hallmarks of evidence-based practice, and has been strongly influenced by research that aims to test effectiveness through experiments. In this chapter we take a different approach. Some influential social work writers believe that experimental studies of intervention, using quantitative methods, are the best, perhaps only trustworthy way of identifying the outcomes of social work. Thyer and Fischer in the USA and Macdonald and Sheldon in the UK have been associated with this position. Some writers take a further step and argue that a corresponding logic and approach is needed by social workers in their direct practice – i.e. they believe that social work ought to be like scientific research in its logic and aims. This is sometimes represented through using what are usually called single system designs (e.g. Kazi 1998; Bloom 1993, 1999).

We take a broader view. In this chapter we outline an approach to an evidenced, understanding and just practice that embeds qualitative methods 'translated' and 'inhabited' for the purposes of practice rather than research.

Three aspects of the approach need emphasizing. First, evaluating in practice is not about the application of research findings to practice but about the *method* of enquiry and evaluation. We may label this the difference between research as a 'source' for practice and research as a 'model' for practice. Second, evaluating in practice is a cluster of practice skills and not research skills as such. Third, our orientation draws primarily on the rich literature and practice of *qualitative* enquiry and evaluation.

Translating and inhabiting

A demanding set of skills is necessary to achieve this shaping of practice – skills that we convey through the use of metaphors such as 'translation' and 'inhabit' and through ideas of transfer of learning. To inhabit some place does not happen simply by being there. It involves actively making it our home over a period of time. This process can be described as one of 'counter-colonizing' (e.g. Shaw 2010). Implicit in this metaphor is a recognition that social workers often face the dominance of social science and research 'experts' over practice 'beneficiaries', and suggests in a contrary fashion the potential for practice to challenge social science, and thus contest conventional ways of seeing expert/beneficiary relationships. To translate and communicate are equally demanding. Film often illustrates this, in ways comedic (e.g. *Lost in Translation*) or dramatic (e.g. *Babel*). The tasks of translating and inhabiting exemplify that the relationship between doing social work and doing research is one of conjunction but difference.

Practitioners'-eye view

In the opening chapter the authors emphasized the importance of distinguishing different sources of knowledge in social work, and summarized the argument of Pawson and colleagues that there are five sources of knowledge:

- Organizational knowledge, gained from the management of social work and social care.
- Practitioner knowledge gained from the conduct of social work and social care.
- Policy community knowledge present in and gained from the wider policy environment.
- Research knowledge gathered relatively systematically and with a pre-planned design for how the knowledge will be gathered and generated.
- User and carer knowledge, gained from the experience of service use and reflection thereon.
  (Pawson et al. 2003)

Evaluating in practice does not fit exclusively into any one of these, although it is aimed primarily at strengthening practitioner knowledge (cf. White and Riemann, in press). Practitioner knowledge is likely to be partly tacit, and passed on by word of mouth and observation and expertise. Because this is so, we need to understand the realities of day-to-day practice, and to hear accounts of how work is evaluated, rather than impose an abstract framework of evaluation. We can see something of this by attending to some replies given by practitioners when asked to describe their work, and to say how they knew whether it was going well or not.

All the social workers in this research (Shaw and Shaw 1997a, 1997b) distinguished two types of evaluation – 'evaluation proper' on the one hand, and self evaluation of work with service users on the other hand. Evaluation proper, or 'Evaluation with a capital E' as someone labelled it, was the term practitioners used when they wished to refer to evaluation originating in legal or administrative requirements, planned and implemented by senior agency staff, and filtered through line managers. This model was widely regarded as being part of a change in culture in which evaluation has become 'a big buzz word':

Historically I think that Social Services have tended to be 'woolly' and maybe 'airy-fairy'...there was a view of social workers who responded without having any clear strategy...that we were bumbling and not to say incompetent...I think social workers began to wake up to that really, that we have to be more methodical and more exact in our approach. I think that change began to happen about ten years ago.

This model was not rejected by social workers, but it did not relate in an easy fashion to their own practice.

I think there's a lot of people that, when they say 'evaluation' are asking you to evaluate things that are almost unimportant, things that are essentially quantifiable...Nobody ever asks you to evaluate whether what you did was worth doing.

This apparent distinction between evaluation as a species of counting and evaluating as a measure of worth was made by the majority of the people in the research. The latter was typically seen as lacking priority due to the 'tidal wave' of work.

You haven't got the day-to-day emphasis on it...so it's something you have to want to do yourself. In terms of doing your own evaluation, that is something which is purely down to the individual.

Yet social workers did not wish to be complicit in this. For some, at least, evaluation was not simply a matter of evidence, but 'caught up' in issues of belief and values.

For me my evaluating skills are caught up with what I believe, and the reason I believe I am doing this. And why I'm doing this ultimately is because I want to protect and help children and families, and I want them to get a good service.

If this is so, then evaluating in practice is not and should not remain a peripheral aspect of social work. It is partly a matter of how to do evaluating, but it is also about the purpose and value of social work. Evaluating in practice involves a set of commitments that draw partly on reflective practice and partly on respect for the voice and experience of the service user. These entail a commitment to reflexivity, to 'thinking big and doing small', to appreciating the significance of those who are 'outsiders on the inside', and to rendering explicit what we know and do not know.

An example of how aspects of these commitments can be demonstrated may be borrowed from a helpful recommendation about preparing questions for a research interview. McCracken (1988) recommends that long qualitative interviews are preceded by the investigator reviewing his/her personal experience of the topic of interest. This nicely illustrates an example of how qualitative research methods can be translated for practice, and is especially useful when we draw in some way on our personal experience in trying to understand the circumstances and problems facing the person we are about to interview. Eliciting such prior experience has two paradoxically 'opposite' effects. First, 'deep and long-lived familiarity with the culture under study has, potentially, the grave effect of dulling the investigator's powers of observation and analysis', but 'it also has the advantage of giving the investigator an extraordinarily intimate acquaintance with the object of study' (McCracken, 1988: 32). For 'investigator' we can substitute 'practitioner'. Such a cultural review (McCracken's term),

> Calls for minute examination of [our] experience. The investigator must inventory and examine the associations, incidents and assumptions that surround the topic in his or her mind...the object is to draw out of one's own experience the systematic properties of the topic. (p. 32)

In so doing we demonstrate reflexivity and render explicit what we know and do not know. Our experience of applying this exercise is that the hard work of 'inhabiting' this cultural review in a way that provokes strange and challenging perspectives on social work problems is sometimes ducked in exchange for a quick and hence less helpful listing of obvious items.

Evidence, understanding and justice

We opened the chapter by describing evaluating in practice as an evidenced, understanding and just practice. The three principles can be spelt out as follows:
Social workers should practice

1. In the light of the best *evidence* about what works well for service users.
2. So that service users and carers receive service that is fair, *just* and enabling.

A social work student, working in a Social Services Department team, describes the work he undertook with a man and his partner. Gwynn Davies was in hospital at the time the work was referred.

Mr Davies is a 52-year-old man who is registered disabled. He has chronic mobility problems arising from bronchial problems, and needs annual hospitalization to clear his chest of infection. His first marriage ended in divorce and he has been living with Mrs Watkins and her 14-year-old daughter, Stephanie, in her house for the past three and a half years. They live in a South Wales valley town.

Mrs Watkins visited the office in a distressed state, to tell the duty social worker that she was unable to accept Mr Davies back into her home because he repeatedly exposed himself to Stephanie. Mr Davies was interviewed on the ward. The first interview was difficult. He appeared to deny or evade the issues raised by his partner, and found it difficult to accept that Mrs Watkins would not let him return. He made it clear he had no intention of searching for alternative accommodation. He seemed more interested in his weight-lifting prowess, and at one stage removed his shirt to show his body and asked the social worker what age he thought he was.

Subsequent progress over the following days was slow, and goal setting was difficult. Mrs Watkins continued to visit him on the ward and appeared to act as if relations between them were free from problems. The student discussed with Mrs Watkins the mixed messages she was giving to Mr Davies. He and the practice teacher spoke to the child protection team, conveying their serious concern about Stephanie's welfare.

Hospital staff regarded the student's concerns as misplaced and wanted Mr Davies home as soon as possible. This eventually led to communication difficulties between the hospital and the student.

Reluctantly accepting that the relationship had broken down, at least temporarily, Mr Davies was provided with a list of private landlords, and the local authority was notified of his threatened homelessness. A local housing association visited him in hospital. At this period Mr Davies required constant encouragement to undertake tasks for himself, e.g. using the telephone.

The local council offered him a flat, which he refused on the grounds that he could not manage the steps. Medical evidence was obtained, but the Council was not willing to accept that this provided sufficient grounds to make an alternative offer. He then accepted a bedsit letting, and said he intended to keep in touch with the housing association, but was not happy with the outcome of the social work that had been provided.

(This anonymized case history is used with the consent of the practitioner.)

3. So that they, service users, carers and the organizations in which they work gain the capacity to learn about and *understand* both problems and ways in which they can be solved. It should lead to new learning capacity.

The case example on p. 157 helps to make the point. In asking whether this was good practice, the general question is, did the practitioner embed the three practice principles in his work? But we should be more specific. If the concern is about evidence, examples of questions we may have in mind include:

1. Did the student have a clear hypothesis regarding the problem and its solution, which could be tested by the eventual outcome?
2. Was any intervention clearly specified and capable of being measured?
3. Do we know if the outcomes were the result of the student's practice?
4. What would count as evidence of success or otherwise for each of the professionals interested in this case?

If justice issues are in view, questions would include:

1. Did the social worker take seriously the risk of sexual or physical harm to the women involved?
2. Did the intervention give proper recognition to the power differentials, e.g. between those involved in professional relationships, or on the basis of gender?
3. Were the participants able to give feedback on whether their experience of social work had been helpful?
4. Was the service use enabled to collaborate with the social worker in judging whether the intervention had been helpful?

Understanding and learning raise different questions.

1. Did the student explore his own personal knowledge of the problem gained through his own background and life experience?
2. Were there opportunities for those involved to reflect on the *process* of intervention as well as on the *problems*?
3. Were 'lay' explanations of the problem (i.e. those explanations put forward by Stephanie, Mrs Watkins and Gwynn Davies)

treated with equal seriousness as the explanations put forward by professionals?
4. Was evaluation participatory?

How these questions are answered is of course a matter of judgement. But to suggest possible answers to just the third principle, we might conclude that Mr Davies appears to have reached a gradual, unspoken conclusion that it would not be possible for him to resume his relationship with Mrs Watkins and Stephanie where it was left off. This suggests that the work done by the student had an impact on what initially seemed an intractable position. Other aspects were not dealt with clearly. For example, there is not apparent reflection on the student's personal, taken-for-granted knowledge. Neither was there any participatory evaluation. The recognition of lay explanations was difficult, and recognized to be so by the student. There were sharply divergent views between the partners. Also, the student was concerned that the views conveyed by Mrs Watkins may not represent the whole truth about her relationship with Mr Davies. A related issue was the socio-legal context of practice and its influence on practitioners' ability to hear and give weight to lay explanations.

In noting that the student working with Gwynn Davies did not use any participatory evaluation, we are indicating that the work with this case does not illustrate the direct application of qualitative methods. We have outlined one example of such methods, through McCracken's cultural review. In a single chapter we can do little more than provide pointers to the rich opportunities for developing evaluating in practice. It will require a readiness to explore literature that rarely appears on the reading lists of social work programmes. In Table 8.1 we have suggested starter reading for each practice method. This is perhaps the core resource in this chapter. But of course, the references are offered as resource materials where the work of inhabiting and translating usually remains to be done by the reader.

Self observation

The idea of systematic self observation yields one example where the writers themselves sense that some degree of transfer may be feasible. Rodriguez and Ryave (2002) explore the use of 'systematic self-observation' (SSO) as a research strategy. As a qualitative research tool they see SSO as training informants 'to observe and record a selected feature of their everyday experience' (p. 2). The focus is on understanding the ordinary, in particular the covert, the elusive and

Table 8.1: Methods and Resources for Evaluating in Practice

Qualitative Methods	Resources
Ethnography	Riemann, 2005
Autoethnography	White, 2001
Life history; [auto]biography	Bowen, 1993; Clandinin and Connelly, 1994; Thompson and Holland, 2005
Documents	Prior, 2003; Shaw, 1996: 151–157
Focus Groups	Bond, 1990–91; Shaw, 1996: 158–161; Zeller, 1993
Narrative	McLeod, 1997; Neander and Stott, 2006; Riessman and Quinney, 2005; Wahlström, 2006
Qualitative interviews	Butler, 1996; Holstein and Gubrium, 1995; McCracken, 1988; McPherson, Hunter and McKeganey 1986; Scourfield, 2001
Participant observation	Corsaro, 1985; Fine and Sandström, 1988; Mandell, 1988; Shaw, 1996: 135–141
Participatory inquiry	Forbat and Atkinson, 205; Kearney and Hyle, 2004; Traylen, 1994; Whitmore, 1994 and 2001
Self-observation	Rodriguez and Ryave, 2002
Simulations	Wasoff and Dobash, 1992 and 1996.
Visual methods	Mitchell, forthcoming

the personal. In an effort to overcome the 'numbness to the details of everyday life' (p. 4) respondents are asked to observe 'a single, focused phenomenon that is natural to the culture, is readily noticeable, is intermittent…is bounded…and is of short duration' (p. 5) and also to focus on the subjective.

The recording involves writing a narrative about the situation, the participants, what occurred, the words spoken and thoughts/feelings experienced at the time (i.e. not retrospectively), and doing it as soon as possible after the event. In observing they are instructed in no way to act differently than usual, to never produce instances nor to judge the propriety of the action – 'do not judge it, do not slow down, do not speed up, do not change it, do not question it – just observe it' (p. 17). They refer to a key skill as gaining a 'new mindfulness' about everyday life. In their own studies they have used the method to research telling lies, telling secrets in everyday life, withholding compliments and the role of envy in making social comparisons in everyday life.

Rodriguez and Ryave suggest that their approach might have an application within therapy in that:

- Naming something can help.
- The task of observing without judging 'accesses the roots of the trouble in the tacit dimension' (p. 57) e.g. by identifying triggers/ antecedents to problem behaviour, etc.
- The write-up can act as therapeutic 'time-out'.
- Submitting data to others is a public 'owning up'.
- Sharing with others who are doing the same activity gives a sense of not being alone with a problem.

They are being speculative, not having tried it in this way – and so am I. But we would suggest a wider potential use, and one that adopts a social systems perspective and does not assume the 'client' is simply a target for change. Compared with the single system designs for evaluating intervention that we alluded to at the beginning of this chapter, systematic self observation may well be a preferred component of evaluating-in-practice in two respects:

- It would allow a more contextualized and richer understanding of the nature of a problem in a service user's life, as part of an assessment and planning process.
- Single system approaches are committed to behavioural approaches that typically proceed by counting and measuring incidence and prevalence of problems. SSO is, as we have noted 'more appropriate for the study of hidden or elusive domains, like the motives, memories, thought processes, withheld actions, thoughts and/or emotions that accompany overt behaviours' (p. 11).

We have expanded two examples of evaluating in practice – a cultural review and systematic self observation. The application of the cultural review was to the practitioner, whereas the illustration of SSO was primarily focused on the service user. Evaluating in practice applies equally to both. This kind of practice evaluation and enquiry is not a solitary activity, but one that readily involves communities of practice. Peter Reason's cycles of action and enquiry can be seen in this context (e.g. Reason 1994). Hilary Traylen, for example, drew on Reason's work and offers a model of practice that has clear applications to evaluation and team work in social work (Traylen 1994). She undertook a co-operative enquiry project with health visitors, in which five health visitors met with her monthly over approximately nine months, to address issues of hidden agenda in their practice, which were not revealed when they visited families. They decided to work on how they might appropriately confront families. Over the cycles of participatory work they heard each others' methods, agreeing and refining enquiry methods to be adopted in their own visits, and then applied them in the action phases of the cycle. The method owes something to models of action research. The approach – like any evaluating in practice – is not easy. The practitioners were heavily preoccupied in the early months with action rather than the enquiry process, and found it took some time to achieve the best balance between the two. However, reflection revealed the centrality of story-telling methods and the empowering impact of each cycle of enquiry.

Developing good practice

We have suggested several ways through which good evaluating in practice can be developed. They can be summarized as six working rules that draw to varying degrees on the principles regarding evidence, justice and understanding. First, concentrated critical reflection on our own practice is essential. This will include close attention to how we describe practice and people, and the relationship of that description to planned and actual outcomes.

Second, to repeat an earlier point, practitioners must come to know what they know. They must work to elicit, where possible, their tacit, taken-for-granted knowledge, and assess its relevance, for good or ill, for their practice. Some forms of tacit knowledge can probably be made explicit, but others are by their nature tacit. This is not a psychodynamic model of unconscious knowledge, but a sociological way of thinking about knowledge.This will include the reviewing of personal and cultural knowledge that we have described. But it will also include acting on the wider applications of the insistence of, e.g. black feminist writers, that black women must 'learn to trust their own personal and cultural biographies as significant sources of knowledge' (Collins 1986: 29). This is a difficult balancing act. On the one hand we should aim constantly to falsify our hunches and hypotheses, by watching for evidence that will help question conclusions arrived at too conveniently. On the other hand, there is a danger we may become paralysed into inaction by the uncertainty of our understanding. Reid has suggested that, if practitioners focus their energies on the achievement of effective but probably modest results from intervention research, this can 'discourage more radical but possibly less testable innovations'. He goes on to ask, 'Is it better to make limited but well documented progress or to work towards more important goals with less certainty of that we have attained?' (Reid 1988: 45).

Third, practitioners must begin with the knowledge that service users and carers bring to them. This means more than listening to service user views, important and inescapably unsettling as that must always prove. It also includes openness to a view of the world that may be entirely at odds with our preconceptions.

Fourth, practitioners should exploit the implications of the analogy between some research methods and direct practice methods. We have sketched examples in this chapter of how this can be done through a process of translating and inhabiting qualitative research and evaluation methods. We have assumed, though not said, that qualitative methods offer a rich seam of work that will challenge social work to a much wider vision of practice-relevance. Social work is perhaps best seen as a field of study and a profession that draws on ideas and knowledge from a range of other disciplines – psychology, social policy, sociology, law, and medicine to instance an incomplete list.

Fifth, evaluating in practice requires a model of team and colleague work. We noted Hilary Traylen's use of Reason's model of participatory enquiry that involves successive cycles of enquiry and action.

The sixth working rule is that practitioners must engage in participatory evaluation with service users. As first steps to achieving this, social workers must insert themselves in the other's story as a way of coming to know that story. Whitmore's compelling accounts of participatory enquiry with oppressed black women and with young people, and Martin's reviews of feminist participatory research demonstrate both the rewards and difficulties of doing so (Martin 1994; Whitmore 1994, 2001).

Whitmore's account of an evaluation of a pre-natal programme for single expectant mothers was carried out over several months by four women who had themselves been through the programme, with Whitmore as consultant to the project. There were tensions in the group. One member left, and there were communication problems. One participant protested to Whitmore that

> Our world is different from yours. The fear is that people always want to humiliate you, put you down...We have a different lifestyle from you. We just don't trust people the way you do. (Whitmore 1994: 92)

But the strength of their final achievement, leading also to presentations to the project advisory group, a conference, and a university class, was evidence that participatory evaluation with oppressed groups goes beyond rhetoric. A consideration arising from this kind of work arises from the recognition of feminist analysis that there is no single women's experience which transcends boundaries of class, race, education and language. Whitmore concluded that she could never entirely share the worlds of the women with whom she worked. 'My small words were often their big words. What I assumed was "normal talk" they saw as "professor words"' (p. 92).

These working rules clearly owe debts to the 'tripod' of evidence, understanding and justice. Tacit knowledge with its links to understanding; the service user's voice, and participatory enquiry take us back to justice; falsifying our prior assumptions borrows the ideas of the philosopher Karl Popper, and demands evidential standards. Developing evaluating in practice is part of a wider agenda. During this book we have found it impossible to avoid mention of important controversies about the nature and purpose of social work. 'Is social work primarily a technology-driven methodology, or is it a set of ideas, values and beliefs, about individuals and society?' (Witkin 1992: 267). Our answer is the one that Witkin gives. Evaluating in practice is not limited to determining whether practice is effective, but must also be a means of empowerment and social change. 'By oversubscribing to the empirical model, we risk valuing effectiveness questions over moral ones, goal achievement over goal worthiness, and empirical data over personal lived experience' (p. 267). Evaluating in practice challenges social work students and practitioners to new understandings and new methodology. It recognizes throughout the significance of workers' present evaluating-as-it-is practices. Most importantly, it holds the promise of keeping social work honest.

Conclusion

We began this book by introducing a 'confounding variable' – 'commonplace complexity' – which renders the search for truth and certainty problematic in practice, and which necessitated an excursion into philosophical territory as we sought to make sense of the implications of this practice context for what we might 'know' in social work. In Chapter 1, we reviewed the relationship between debates in the philosophy of science regarding the nature and status of knowledge and the forms of knowledge utilized in social work. In particular, the defining characteristics and associated strengths and weaknesses of alternative paradigms were outlined. SCIE's influential knowledge typology was highlighted as an organizing framework for the chapters which followed. The competing perspectives in this debate were further delineated via exploration – and problematization – of the notion of evidence-based social work in Chapter 2. In Chapter 3, through discussion of service user knowledge, the potential that informal knowledge sources might offer as a counterbalance to more dominant formal knowledge was highlighted. The ways in which the status of forms of knowledge reflects the power and position of respondents were emphasized. This issue was contextualized and further developed by discussion of research knowledge and how this might be assessed and used in practice in Chapter 4. The particular issues associated with knowledge generated in policy contexts, particularly the operation of professional discretion, were elaborated on in Chapter 5, while the relevance of such debates to the 'nuts and bolts' of practice was explored through discussion of the distinctiveness of alternative 'versions' of practitioner knowledge in Chapter 6. Chapters 7 and 8 specified how social workers and agencies might actualize many of these issues via the notions of 'the learning organization' and 'evaluating in practice'.

As we approach the end of this book, then, it should be clear that there are multiple, sometimes complementary but often competing perspectives regarding forms of knowledge in social work and how these should be generated, assessed and applied if they are to be relevant and useful for practitioners and for social work more broadly. The status of social work as a 'public good' is threatened, given the seemingly deep-seated view that service 'failures' are indicative of ingrained disciplinary incompetence and that social work is neither effective or just in the contribution it makes to remedying societal ills. Various strategies have been advanced to address this legitimacy gap. Under evidence-based social work, practitioner discretion is problematized. Advocates of reduced discretion see this as a necessary component of a move away from authority-based practice to evidence-based practice. After all, it is the existence of discretion which enables practitioners to disregard the findings of research and work according to their own interpretations and preferences. On the other hand, supporters of reflective practice regard the very existence of discretion as the basis for positive potential in practice. Without discretion to choose how to react in particular circumstances, practitioners are left with little scope for creativity, which is regarded as essential if the unique characteristics of service users are to be responded to constructively.

As we have seen, there are affiliations between these strategies and particular paradigmatic positions, which themselves represent statements regarding the nature and status of knowledge and around which controversies abound. What is apparent is that many of the debates that arise are enduring, and they are enduring because they are probably irresolvable. Despite – or maybe because of – this, nevertheless there is sufficient overlap between alternative perspectives to prompt optimism regarding the potential for rapprochement. There are pressing reasons why this ought to be pursued. As we have stressed, the stakes are high in social work, and the threats it faces substantial. Whichever 'version' of social work is subscribed to, there is little to be gained from unnecessarily exacerbating internal divisions. Specifying the basis on which bridges may be built, then, is an important and necessary task and so in this concluding chapter, we explore the potential of an approach which thus far we have barely touched upon in encouraging some degree of disciplinary convergence. After all, what is apparent is that despite their divergent positions regarding the nature, objectives and methods of social work, and particular paradigmatic preferences, all of the 'combatants' within the skirmishes we have reported on nevertheless share a commitment to ensuring that the quality of social work practice is as good as it possibly can be. They differ only in their varying specifications as to the means via which this might be achieved.

Moving forward

It does seem to us that common-place complexity renders the straightforward application of experimentally developed knowledge to many practice scenarios problematic. Critical realists explain why such generalization is not necessarily possible in terms of the unique properties of the variables in the equation 'outcome = mechanism + context'. Interpretivists suggest that it is because much of practice concerns subjectively experienced moral and ethical dilemmas in conditions of inherent uncertainty, meaning that practitioners are not able to rely on existing knowledge to resolve the dilemmas with which they are confronted. Critical theorists, meanwhile, draw our attention to the meaningful effect that political, rather than empirical considerations have in determining practice and its outcomes. Cumulatively, these perspectives represent a real challenge to the claims of advocates of evidence-based social work. At the same time, however, each of these alternatives has their own limitations, not least their potential complexity, relativism and bias, respectively, which arguably inhibit attempts to specify the basis of good, effective social work practice and the development of a professional knowledge base. Being aware of the limitations of experimental method, then, is not the same as demonstrating that it has nothing of value to contribute.

We have also seen that despite the rhetoric, in absolute terms, many of the disagreements which characterize philosophical and methodological debate are ersatz – not real. As Reid puts it, 'when one steps behind the rhetorical and epistemological screens of alternative approaches, one finds...that they have much in common' (2001: 287). The debate between proponents of alternative positions is sometimes characterized by misrepresentation of alternative viewpoints. Are there really any experimental researchers in the social sciences who subject service users to fiendish experiments with no concern for their thoughts, feelings and wishes? Are strong advocates of social constructionism or post-modernism evident in social work practice, which actually tends to reflect broadly realist principles, including that certain courses of action – neglect of a child, for example – do have harmful effects, and that we can and should act to limit or prevent these? Those informed by critical theory also take this position – indeed, it is awareness of the meaningful effects of oppressive actions and situations on the lived reality of those so affected which drives their commitment to change. These clear linkages tend to be downplayed rather than highlighted. Howe suggests that 'reconciliation...is difficult as each believes that to admit too much interest in the ideas of the other is to sup with the devil' (2009: 197). We agree, but see some potential for moving forward. Key here is the potential that the relatively neglected pragmatic philosophical position offers as a basis for practice.

Bridging the gap

We have mentioned at various points in this book that philosophical argument, though central to understanding the relationship between knowledge and practice, can appear distant from day-to-day social work. There are good reasons for this, not least that these are distinct activities. 'Theorists' are concerned with articulating normative ideals about what practice 'should' be seeking to achieve. Practitioners, however, have a specific job to do, reflecting a judgement which has been made within these debates. Moreover, consequently they are aware of the limits of idealism, not least its potential to limit action. Arguably, practice invariably involves navigating a course between the ideal and the possible. After all, if we lived in an ideal world, there would be no need for social workers! In our view insufficient attention has been paid to the complexities of the relationship between the pragmatic processes whereby decision-making and actions are undertaken, and the philosophy of pragmatism.

There is a mistaken but seemingly common belief in social work that almost by definition, pragmatic practice must be unprincipled, and that for a value-driven profession this represents a threat rather than a potentially constructive contribution. This is not necessarily the case. It seems to us that for better or worse, much of what social workers do occurs within less than ideal circumstances, and that part and parcel of what it is to be an effective practitioner is concerned with negotiating the 'trade off' between what should be and what can be. Rather than viewing this as problematic, as idealists often do (Lymbery and Butler 2004) there seems much scope for learning more about 'what works' in dealing with commonplace complexity if attention is focused upon the positive outcomes that often result when practitioners engage in situated decision-making and problem-solving in complex scenarios. After all, though critics of social work routinely question the competence of social workers, it is clear that much practice *is* effective. To disregard how practitioners make things work on a day-to-day basis would be a major omission. Pragmatic philosophy offers potential as a framework for making sense of practice which is suited to the actual – rather than idealized – nature of social work.

Pragmatism

Like all philosophical schools, pragmatism is a broad church which accommodates diverse perspectives. Here we will focus on key tenets and their relationship to alternative perspectives which we have already covered.

Generally, pragmatists see little merit in pursuing notions of essential truth, whereby knowledge is a representation of some inner essence. Instead, knowledge is seen as a practical vehicle for problem-solving. It is informed by science, but nevertheless sceptical about the status of scientific method and findings as either privileged or final. Given that the history of human experience testifies to the inability of any system of enquiry or explanation to provide global answers to life's questions, pragmatists assume that the prospects of the transcendental search for truth providing unshakeable knowledge are poor – 'the search for a single method that guarantees progress is a wild goose chase' (Baert 2003: 96). This is because, although reality has substance (and so pragmatists are ontologically realist), it is in a constant state of change, which renders 'final answers' problematic. Consequently, they urge a shift in focus from 'pointless exercises' – those metaphysical debates and arguments which are irresolvable – to activity which is likely to have change-related effect. There is also a distinctive emphasis on assessing the status of a knowledge claim according to its usefulness in 'getting the job done'. Here, then, there is a concern with action and praxis.

Pragmatists are sceptical regarding adherence to a particular method as a means of producing useful knowledge (knowledge which assists in the furtherance of a specified aim) and this scepticism applies to all approaches, quantitative or qualitative, positivist or interpretive, realist or constructionist. As such, pragmatists look to make use of methods which appear best suited to the task in hand,

and move on to develop and try alternative arrangements where initial options are unsuccessful, rather than insisting that authority or expertise hold sway. In this respect, they have no fixed theoretical or methodological allegiances, reflecting their belief that neither knowledge or the purposes to which it is put is static, and so theory and method will have to change to reflect these variable contexts. The utility of knowledge is therefore assessed according to its adequacy rather than absolute criteria – whether it is 'good enough', rather than a precise mirroring of reality (Rorty 1979).

The pragmatic approach is underpinned by a commitment to 'changing one's mind', a form of reflexivity whereby, rather than being committed to particular epistemological or methodological approaches, 'the encounter with different practices or beliefs forces us to reflect and alter our presuppositions' (Baert 2003: 102). Here, pragmatists are distancing themselves from the sometime tendency in the social sciences for researchers to undertake studies which confirm their pre-existing views or allegiances (Baert 2004). If the purpose of research is to produce useful knowledge which will enable us to move forward, there is little value in reiterating what is already 'known', and much to be gained where we approach such endeavour with 'the necessary willingness to be surprised and affected by what is being studied' (Baert 2003: 104).

There are clearly echoes here of the 'mixed-method' research we referred to in Chapter 4, which on the one hand offer the potential to overcome the limitations of one approach via the utilization of the strengths of another, but also attract criticism for downplaying the importance of coherence between paradigmatic assumptions and method. Pragmatic philosophy does not render such concerns null and void. It does, however, suggest that where the purpose of knowledge is to inform practice (as is the case with social work), there is much to be gained from suspending undue reflection in favour of action, and offers a model for doing so.

A pragmatic philosophy of practice

The implications of a pragmatic philosophy for practice have been elaborated on by Polkinghorne (2004), who has applied John Dewey's 'theory of learning from practice' (where 'practice' refers to the living of everyday life) to the caring professions. Dewey's particular concern was with improvements in practical knowledge that come about as a result of 'after the fact' thought regarding the failure of existing knowledge to successfully contribute to the achievement of intended objectives. Much of the knowledge which informs the choices we make in deciding how to act in life is tacit, based upon our background and experiences, and most of the time this is sufficient for our needs. However, in certain circumstances – 'indeterminate situations' – our existing knowledge is insufficient and we are unable to achieve our aims. What follows is a process of reflective learning and enquiry geared to problem-solving, to transforming an indeterminate scenario into a determinate one.

It begins with the careful consideration of why ordinary ways of acting were insufficient on this occasion, the specification of the problem to be solved. This is followed by the generation of alternative ideas which might solve the problem. These ideas are unproblematically conceived of as hypotheses, betraying a debt to logical positivism, to be tested through application in action. However, there is acceptance of the value of analogy and metaphor – or imagination – as a basis for their generation, rather than insistence that these must arise from existing theory. The testing of hypotheses occurs in their application to the identified problem in practice. If it is effective – 'good enough' to enable movement towards the original aim – then all well and good, at least for now. If ineffective, the enquiry process continues, with successive hypotheses tested until a workable solution is arrived at. This will be a situated solution, in line with the pragmatic recognition that knowledge is not fixed or stable. Pragmatists do not go as far as some critical realists in suggesting that knowledge is unique to a particular configuration of mechanism and context – an assertion which in its extreme form inhibits any generalization beyond the unique interaction concerned. Instead generalization may be possible, but changing circumstances render assertions of solid knowledge foundations vulnerable. Consequently, Dewey's concerns are not as grand as the nature of reality and how this might be known, but instead 'finding solutions to problems through experimentation in the real world' (Polkinghorne 2004: 122).

These ideas may not appear radically different from many of the models we have already discussed – reflection 'on' action, critical incident analysis, and the notion of the learning agency all utilize similar processes, while the realist evaluation 'cycle' and hypotheses generation and testing are premised upon similar assumptions. Additionally, the process specified here seems to match quite closely the way that practitioners *actually go about* their work, and in terms of social work models and processes, is not dissimilar to the logic and process associated with task-centred practice. Baert (2003) points to links between pragmatism and many influential thinkers and schools within social science, suggesting that this is because pragmatic thought has been influential without necessarily being acknowledged. This is especially the case in social work, perhaps because of the mistaken assumption that in rejecting a commitment to a particular standpoint, pragmatism is incompatible with principled, emancipatory forms of practice. And indeed, pragmatists would be sceptical about the status of claims to knowledge which reify particular values without attention being paid to their contemporary adequacy, on the basis that the circumstances which gave rise to the need for their development in the first place are likely to have subsequently changed. Nevertheless, it is clear that pragmatic method supplements rather than supplants ethical deliberation, in that, though its concerns may be situated, they occur within the context of a commitment to the notion of action as a means to a particular end, which is 'what is best in a particular situation for a particular person' (Polkinghorne 2004: 123).

There are increasing signs of an awareness of the need to ensure that discussion of the links between knowledge and practice accommodates the practical nature of social work and thus the potential of pragmatism. There is indeed a need for a philosophy of practice which is meaningful, adequate and useful, and which sidesteps some of the irresolvable tensions inherent in paradigmatic debate. We concur with Panaser who suggests that 'what we need now is a pragmatic realism that suggests that social work can help to change things for the better, but that there are some things that we cannot change' (2003: 115). A pragmatic approach has been defined – not uncritically – as one which is 'mindful of the realities and constraints of professional social work practice' (Gray et al. 2009: 60). It emphasizes the value of knowledge which is useful, applicable to the task of making judgements about how to act in specific contexts, and evaluated according to its strengths and weaknesses in furthering practice objectives. 'Mixed methods' are advocated as best placed to generate knowledge which accommodates the complexities of practice. Both Reid (2001) and Shaw (1999) are seen as exemplifying this approach (whether either would self refer is debatable) in their emphasis on generating knowledge which is specific to organizational requirements by integrating outcome data derived from experimental evaluation with practice wisdom and service user feedback.

Reid and Shaw are both sceptical regarding the claims of any particular paradigm or method to produce definitive knowledge whose nature and status is beyond contestation. Despite this, they nevertheless see value in the utility of the notion of 'truth' as an 'orientating device': 'truth can be a regulative ideal, a goal that we strive for but do not always attain. We must often settle for probabilistic, approximate or partial truths' (Reid 2001: 276). Although 'ultimate' truth may be unachievable, partial truths, the best approximations possible under existing conditions, are adequate or 'good enough'. It is also 'premature to rally around one particular flag' (Shaw and Gould 2001: 4) and discount the value of knowledge generated within any particular paradigmatic or methodological tradition. The implications of this position, then, are that in practice, decision-making will be on the basis of the 'balance of evidence' generated from multiple sources and paradigms. It is unavoidable that such decisions will involve differentiating between competing claims based on less than full knowledge. Practitioners therefore have no option but to make judgements and act pragmatically.

Though we advocate a pragmatic approach as a basis for rapprochement, it does not, of course, resolve all tensions and dilemmas. There are various points of contention. The pragmatic problem-solving process assumes that 'progress' will occur cumulatively and in this sense it is resolutely modernist. As such, it is unlikely to satisfy those critics – such as Humphries (2008) – who are alert to attempts to 'smuggle' positivist assumptions into social work research, nor those post-modernists who see modernity and interpretivism as antithetical. However its objectives are not absolute, given the caveat that knowledge be 'good enough', and so such concerns may be mitigated to some extent. Next, it is clearly at odds with 'not knowing' a popular position in response to increased awareness that social work is characterized by uncertainty, ambiguity and complexity.Whereas some have welcomed this, pragmatists see uncertainty as a starting point – a problem to work towards providing workable, practical solutions to, rather than an insurmountable difficulty which we have no option but to celebrate. Finally, Gray et al. have suggested that pragmatism promotes an 'anything goes' approach to research method and practice and so there is a 'risk that pragmatic evidence-based social work will become an excuse to ignore research altogether' (2009: 63). This is a concern shared by Guba and Lincoln, who have characterized problem rather than paradigm driven research as 'mindless'. Shaw in particular is alert to the need to guard against this tendency, and sees no necessary contradiction in integrating criteria of rigour and relevance with knowledge drawn from multiple sources.

Despite these tensions, we do nevertheless take the view that it is around the 'reality' of social work endeavour that future debates about knowledge and practice should focus and that, on balance, compared to alternative options, a pragmatic philosophy of practice both fits more coherently with the actual nature of social work practice and offers more potential for links to develop between competing camps. There is much to be gained from further development of this perspective. Howe makes convincing case as to why this might be: 'Pragmatic social work...is happy to both deduce and induce, to make interventions backed by good research evidence but also to take actions that require judgements backed by sound values' (2009: 205). Put another way, it entails both art and science, because the nature of the problems which social workers need to address are such that neither science nor art are in themselves adequate. There is recognition that formal knowledge has value, but also that 'judgements without evidence will remain the reality of much social work practice that deals with unique, dynamic and complex scenarios' (Gray et al. 2009: 63). As such, it is not viable to separate formal and informal knowledge sources, as each has something valuable to contribute to decision-making and action. Pragmatism is therefore well placed to take a meaningful role as a philosophy for practice which has the potential to 'bridge the gap' between art and science. It is also (relatively) practical, which is helpful given the commonplace complaint of practitioners that much social work theorizing is distant from their day-to-day concerns. Too much philosophizing can distract from the task at hand. At the end of the day (and often earlier!) social workers need to make decisions and intervene. Perhaps a philosophy which shares these imperatives represents a fitting basis for their actions. A pragmatic philosophy of practice – oriented towards making decisions and acting based upon the most reasonable option in a given case – would seem to represent a reasonable way forward. It might not provide a means of answering all of the questions which practitioners must address, but, as we hope we have demonstrated in this book, that would be an untenable claim for the advocates of any philosophy of practice to make. In the absence of unassailable evidence regarding what works for whom in which circumstances and why, this seems an eminently reasonable basis on which to proceed.

In this book we have sought to do justice to the complexity of debates concerning the relationship between knowledge, evidence and practice. We have also been aware of the need to 'translate' what can seem complex, esoteric and abstract ideas and concepts so that they are meaningful and relevant to an informed audience. Whether we have achieved an appropriate balance between these dual imperatives will be for individual readers to judge. What is hopefully clear, however, is that debates about knowledge, evidence and practice are as much to do with the practicalities of social work as they are with ethics and values. Where we differ from some 'voices' in this debate is in our recognition that there are limits to idealism, which in itself is insufficient as a basis for meeting contemporary challenges. Uncertainty may be unavoidable in contemporary social work practice, but knowledge and evidence offer some potential to limit its effects. Practitioners have no option but to make decisions and act as though these choices are objective, knowing full well that the knowledge upon which they are based is often contested and so their judgements and actions may be 'wrong'. This is a difficult position, but one which practitioners navigate relatively well, as is evident when the successes, rather than the failures of social work are considered. This, it seems to us, is an optimistic point at which to end, with a 'version' of social work knowledge which reflects the reality of social work practice. It also has the advantage of reminding us that the limits of social work reflect the limits of knowledge itself.

References

Aldridge, M. (1996) 'Dragged to market: being a profession in the post-modern world', *British Journal of Social Work*, 26, 177–94.

Alvesson, M. (2002) *Post-Modernism and Social Research*, London: Sage.

Baert, P. (2003) 'Pragmatism, realism and hermeneutics', *Foundations of Science*, 8, 89–106.

(2004) 'Pragmatism as a philosophy of the social sciences', *European Journal of Social Theory*, 7, 355–69.

Banks, S. (2006) *Ethics and Values in Social Work*, Basingstoke: Palgrave Macmillan.

Barnes, C. (1996) 'Disability and the myth of the independent researcher', *Disability and Society*, 11, 107–10.

(2003) 'What a difference a decade makes: reflections on doing "emancipatory" disability research', *Disability and Society*, 18, 3–17.

Barnes, C. and Mercer, G. (1997) 'Breaking the mould? An introduction to doing disability research' in Barnes, C. and Mercer, G. (eds) *Doing Disability Research*, Leeds: The Disability Press.

Barret, S. and Fudge, C. (eds) (1981) *Policy and Action*, London: Methuen.

Barret, S. and Hill, M. (1984) 'Policy, bargaining and structure in implementation theory: towards an integrated perspective', *Policy and Politics*, 12, 219–40.

BASW (2002) *Code of Ethics*, Birmingham: BASW.

Becker, H. (1967) 'Whose side are we on?', *Social Problems*, 239, 239–47.

(1993) 'Theory: the necessary evil', in D. Flinders and G. Mills (eds) *Theory and Concepts in Qualitative Research: Perspectives from the Field*, New York: Columbia University Press.

Bhaskar, R. (1997) *A Realist Theory of Science*, London: Version.

Blackburn, S. (2005), *Oxford Dictionary of Philosophy*, Oxford: Oxford University Press.

Blaikie, N. (2007) *Approaches to Social Enquiry*, Cambridge: Polity.

Bloom, M. (1993) (ed.) *Single System Designs in the Social Services*, New York: Haworth.

(1999) 'Single system evaluation' in Shaw, I. and Lishman, J. (eds) *Evaluation and Social Work Practice*, London: Sage.

Bond, M. (1990–1) ' "The centre, it's for children": seeking children's views as users of a family centre', *Practice*, 7 (2).

Bortolotti, L. (2008) *An Introduction to the Philosophy of Science*, Cambridge: Polity.

Bowen, D. (1993) 'The delights of learning to apply the life history method to school non-attenders' in Broad, B. and Fletcher, C. (eds) *Practitioner Social Work Research in Action*, London: Whiting and Birch.

Bradley, G. (2003) 'Administrative justice and charging for care', *British Journal of Social Work*, 33, 641–57.

Bradshaw, W. (2003) 'Use of single system research to evaluate the effectiveness of cognitive-behavioural treatment of schizophrenia', *British Journal of Social Work*, 5, 885–99.

Brewer, C. and Lait, J. (1980) *Can Social Work Survive?*, London: Maurice Temple Smith.

Brindle, D. (2008) 'We must be wary of cost-cutting' *Guardian*: Society Section, 6 Feb., p. 5.

Butler, A. (2005) 'A strengths approach to building futures: UK students and refugees together', *Community Development Journal*, 40, 147–57.

(2007) 'Students and refugees together: towards a model of practice learning as service provision', *Social Work Education*, 26, 233–46.

(2008) Personal Communication, 14 April 2008.

Butler, I. and Williamson, H. (1996) ' "Safe?" Involving children in child protection' in Butler, I. and Shaw, I. (eds) *A Case of Neglect? Children's Experience and the Sociology of Childhood*, Aldershot: Avebury.

Cabinet Office (1999) *The Modernising Government*, London: Cabinet Office.

Chambers, R. 'Professionalism in social work' in Wootton, B. (1959) *Social Science and Social Pathology*, London: Allen and Unwin.

Children Act 1989, 2004.

Clandinin, J. and Connelly, M. (1994) 'Personal experience methods' in Denzin, N. and Lincoln, Y. (eds) *Handbook of Qualitative Research*, Thousand Oaks: Sage.

Cohen-Mitchell, J. (2000) 'Disabled women in El Salvador reframing themselves: an economic development program for women' in Truman, C., Mertens, D. and Humphries, B. (eds) *Research and Inequality*, London: UCL Press.

Collins, P. (1986) 'Learning from the outsider within: the sociological significance of black feminist thought' in *Social Problems*, 33 (6).

Cook-Craig, P. G. and Sabah, Y. (2009) 'The role of virtual communities of practice in supporting collaborative learning among social workers' in *British Journal of Social Work*, 39 (4): 725–39.

Corby, B. (2006) *Applying Research in Social Work Practice*, Maidenhead: Open University Press.

Corsaro, W. (1985) *Friendship and Peer Culture in Early Years*, Norwood, N J: Ablex.

Cozens, A. (2008) 'Poor Law care due for an upgrade', *Guardian*: Society Section, 6 Feb., p. 2.

Cree, V. (2002) 'The changing nature of social work', in R. Adams, L. Dominelli and M. Payne (eds) *Social work: Themes, Issues and Critical Debates*, Basingstoke: Palgrave Macmillan.

Critical Social Policy (2006) Special Issue on Devolution: issue 88.

D'Cruz, H. and Jones, M. (2003) *Social Work Research: Ethical and Political Contexts*, London: Sage.

Daly, E. and Ballantyne, N. (2009) 'Retelling the past using new technologies: a case study into the digitization of social work heritage material and the creation of a virtual exhibition', *Journal of Technology in Human Services*, 27 (1): 44–56.

Dartington, T., Miller, E., and Gwynne, G. (1981) *A Life Together*, London: Tavistock Publications.

Davidoff, F., Haynes, B., Sackett, D., and Smith, R. (1995) 'Evidence-based medicine', *British Medical Journal*, 310, 6987.

Davis, K. (1971) *Discretionary Justice: A Preliminary Inquiry*, Urbana, Ill.: University of Illinois Press.

Delanty, G. and Strydom, P. (2003) *Philosophies of Social Science – The Classic and Contemporary Readings*, Maidenhead: Open University Press.

Department for Education and Skills (2003) *Every Child Matters*, London: Department for Education and Skills.

Department of Health (1998) *Modernising Social Services: Promoting Independence, Improving Protection, Raising Standards*, London: HMSO.

(2006) *Our Health, Our Care, Our Say*, London: Department of Health.

(2007) *Modernising Adult Social Care – What's Working*, London: Department of Health.

Derber, C. (1983) 'Managing professionals: ideological proletarianization and post-industrial labor', *Theory and Society*, 12, 309–41.

Dominelli, L. (2005) 'Social work research: contested knowledge for practice' in R. Adams, L. Dominelli and M. Payne (eds) *Social Work Futures*, Basingstoke: Palgrave Macmillan.

Drakeford, M. (2002) 'Social work and politics' in Davies, M. (ed.) *Blackwell Companion to Social Work*, Oxford: Blackwell.

England, H. (1986) *Social Work as Art – Making Sense for Good Practice*, London: Allen and Unwin.

Evans, T. (2009) 'Managing to be professional? Team managers and practitioners in social services', in Harris, J. and White, V. (eds) *Modernising Social Work*, Bristol: Policy Press.

Evans, T. and Harris, J. (2004) 'Street-level bureaucracy, social work and the (exaggerated) death of discretion', *British Journal of Social Work*, 34, 871–95.

Everitt, A. and Hardiker, P. (1996) *Evaluating for Better Practice*, London: Macmillan.

Everitt, A., Hardiker, P., Littlewood, J., and Mullender, A. (1992) *Applied Research for Better Practice*, London: Macmillan.

Every Child Matters (2008) [online]. Accessed 1 March 2008. Available from World Wide Web: http://www.everychildmatters.gov.uk/socialcare/socialservices/

Evetts, J. (2002) 'New directions in state and international professional occupations: discretionary decision-making and acquired regulation', *Work, Employment and Society*, 16, 341–53.

(2006) 'The Sociology of Professional Groups: New Directions', *Current Sociology*, 54; 133–43.

Evidence-Based Medicine Working Group (1992) 'Evidence-based medicine: a new approach to teaching the practice of medicine', *Journal of the American Medical Association*, 268, 2420–5.

Fawcett, B. (2009) 'Post-modernism', in M. Gray and S. A. Webb (eds) *Social Work Theories and Methods*, London: Sage.

Fine, G. and Sandström, K. (1988) *Knowing Children: Participant Observation with Minors*, Newbury Park: Sage.

Finkelstein, V. (1999) 'Doing disability research', *Disability and Society*, 14, 859–67.

Fisher, M. (2002) 'The Social Care Institute of Excellence: the role of a national institute in developing knowledge and practice in social care', *Social Work and Social Sciences Review*, 10, 6–34.

(2002) 'The role of service users in problem formulation and technical aspects of social research', *Social Work Education*, 21, 305–12.

Fook, J. (2002) *Social Work – Critical Theory and Practice*, London: Sage.

(2007) 'Uncertainty: the defining characteristic of social work?' in M. Lymbery and K. Postle (eds) *Social Work – A Companion to Learning*, London: Sage.

Fook, J. and Gardner, F. (2007) *Practising Critical Reflection – A Resource Handbook*, Maidenhead: Open University Press.

Forbat, E. and Atkinson, D. (2005) 'Research as social work: participatory research in learning disability' in *British Journal of Social Work*, 35 (4): 425–34.

Fournier, V. (1999) The appeal to 'professionalism' as a disciplinary mechanism, *The Sociological Review*, 280–307.

Freidson, E. (2001) *Professionalism: The Third Logic*, Cambridge: Polity.

French, S. (1993) 'Disability, impairment or something in between?' in Swain, J., Finkelstein, V., French, S. and Oliver, M. (eds) *Disabling Barriers-Enabling Environments*, London: Sage.

Gambrill, E. (2006) *Social Work Practice: A Critical Thinker's Guide*, Oxford: Oxford University Press.

General Medical Council (2003) *Tomorrow's Doctors*, London: General Medical Council.

General Social Care Council (2008) *Social Work at its Best: The Roles and Tasks of Social Workers*, London: GSCC.

Gibbs, L., and Gambrill, E. (2002) 'Evidence-based practice: counterarguments to objections', *Research on Social Work Practice*, 12, 252–476.

Giddens, A. (1984) *The Constitution of Society*, Cambridge: Polity.

Gray, M., Plath, D. and Webb, S. A. (2009) *Evidence-Based Social Work – A Critical Stance*, Abingdon: Routledge.

Gray, M. and McDonald, C. (2006) 'Pursuing good practice? The limits of evidence-based practice', *Journal of Social Work*, 6, 7–20.

Greer, S. (2003) 'Will it change something in Greenock?' in Hazell, R. (ed.) *The State of the Nations 2003*, London: Imprint Academic: 196–214.

Grimshaw, J. (1986), *Feminist Philosophers: Women's Perspectives on Philosophical Traditions*, Brighton: Wheatsheaf.

GSCC (2008) *Social Work at its Best: A Statement of Social Work Roles and Tasks for the 21st Century*, London: GSCC.

Guba, E. G. and Lincoln, Y. S. (1982) 'Epistemological and methodological bases of naturalistic inquiry', *Educational Technology Research and Development*, 30, 232–52.

Hall, T. (2001) 'Caught not taught: ethnographic research at a young people's accommodation project' in Shaw, I. and Gould, N. *Qualitative Research in Social Work*, London: Sage.

Hammersley, M. (1995) *The Politics of Social Research*, London: Sage.

Hanley, B. (2005) *Research as Empowerment*, York: Joseph Rowntree Foundation.

Harding, S. (2004) 'Introduction: Standpoint Theory as a Site of Political, Philosophic, and Scientific Data' in Harding, S. (ed.) *The Feminist Standpoint Theory Reader*, New York: Routledge.

Harris, J. (1998) 'Scientific management, bureau-professionalism and new managerialism. The labour process of state social work', *British Journal of Social Work*, 28, 839–62.

— (2008) 'State social work: constructing the present from moments in the past', *British Journal of Social Work*, 38, 662–79.

Harris, N. (1987) 'Defensive social work', *British Journal of Social Work*, 17, 61–9.

Harrison, S., Hunter, D., Marnoch, G. and Pollitt, C. (1992) *Just Managing*, Basingstoke: Macmillan.

Hartsock, N. (2004a) 'The feminist standpoint: developing the ground for a specifically feminist historical materialist' in Harding, S. (ed.) *The Feminist Standpoint Theory Reader*, New York: Routledge.

— (2004b) 'Comment on Heckman's "Truth and method: feminist standpoint theory revisited": truth or justice?' in Harding, S. (ed.) *The Feminist Standpoint Theory Reader*, New York: Routledge.

Healy, K. (2005) *Social work theories in context – creating frameworks for practice*, Basingstoke, Palgrave Macmillan.

Heckman, S. (2004) 'Truth and method: feminist standpoint theory revisited' in Harding, S. (ed.) *The Feminist Standpoint Theory Reader*, New York: Routledge.

Hegel, G. (trans. Miller, A.) (1977) *Phenomenology of Spirit*, Oxford: Oxford University Press.

Hill, M. (2000a) 'The central and local government framework', in M. Hill (ed.), *Local Authority Social Services*, Oxford: Blackwell, 139–57.

(2000b) (ed.), Local Authority Social Services, Oxford: Blackwell.

(2003) Understanding Social Policy, Oxford: Blackwell.

Hogwood, B. and Gunn, L. (1984) *Policy Analysis for the Real World*, Oxford: Oxford University Press.

Holstein, J. and Gubrium, J. (1995) *The Active Interview*, Thousand Oaks: Sage.

Houston, S. (2005) 'Philosophy, theory and method in social work: challenging empiricism's claim on evidence-based practice, *Journal of Social Work*, 5, 7–20.

(2001) 'Beyond social constructionism: critical realism and social work', *British Journal of Social Work*, 31, 845–61.

Howe, D. (1991) 'Knowledge, power and the shape of social work practice' in M. Davies (ed.) *The Sociology of Social Work*, London: Routledge.

(1996) 'Surface and depth in social work practice' in N. Parton (ed.) *Social Theory, Social Change and Social Work*, London: Routledge.

(2009) *A Brief Introduction to Social Work Theory*, Basingstoke: Palgrave Macmillan.

Hudson, B. and Macdonald, G. (1986) *Behavioural Social Work*, Basingstoke, Macmillan.

Hudson, B. and Roberts, C. (1998) 'Teaching social work: a tutor's perspective. Response to Morgan et al.', *Social Work Education*, 17, 153–6.

Hume, D. (1970) *A Treaties of Human Nature: Book One*, London: Fontana.

Humphries, B. (2000) 'From critical thought to emancipatory action: Contradictory research goals?' in Truman, C., Mertens, D. and Humphries, B. (eds) *Research and Inequality*, London: UCL Press.

(2008) *Social Work Research and Social Justice*, Basingstoke: Palgrave Macmillan.

Humphries, B., Mertens, D., and Truman, C. (2000) 'Arguments for an "emancipatory" research paradigm' in Truman, C., Mertens, D. and Humphries, B. (eds) *Research and Inequality*, London: UCL Press.

Hunt, P. (1981) 'Settling accounts with the parasite', *Disability Challenge*, 1, 37–50: http://www.leeds.ac.uk/disability-studies/archiveuk/UPIAS/Disability%20Challenge1.pdf

International Federation of Social Workers (2000) Definition of Social Work [Online]http://www.ifsw.org/f38000138.html Accessed 14 July 2009.

Kanuha, V. K. (2000) 'Being native versus "going native": Conducting social work research as an insider.' *Social Work*, 45 (5), 439–77.

Kazi, M. A. F. (1998) *Single Case Evaluation by Social Workers*, Aldershot: Ashgate.

(2003) *Realist Evaluation in Practice*, London: Sage.

Kearney, K. S. and Hyle, A. E. (2004) 'Drawing out emotions: the use of participant-produced drawings in qualitative inquiry', *Qualitative Research*, 4 (3), 361–82.

Kim, K. and Fox, M. (2006) 'Moving to a holistic model of health among persons with mobility disabilities', *Qualitative Social Work*, 5, 470–88.

Kirk, S. and Reid, W. (2002) *Science and Social Work – A Critical Appraisal*, New York: Columbia University Press.

Kuhn, T. (1970) 'The structure of scientific revolutions', *International Encyclopaedia of Unified Science*, vol. 2, no. 2, Chicago: University of Chicago Press.

LaMendola, W., Ballantyne, and Daly, E. (2009) 'Practitioner networks: professional learning in the twenty-first century' in *British Journal of Social Work*, 39 (4): 710–24.

Latour, B. (1999) *Pandora's Hope: Essays on the Reality of Social Studies*, London: Harvard University Press.

Levine, P. (1997) *Making Social Policy*, Buckingham: Open University Press.

Lewis, J. and Glennerster, H. (1996) *Implementing the New Community Care*, Buckingham: Open University Press.

Lipsky, M. (1980) *Street-level Bureaucracy: The Dilemmas of Individuals in Public Service*, New York: Russell Sage Foundation.

Lunt, N., Shaw, I. and Mitchell, F. (2009) *Practitioner Research in CHILDREN 1st: Cohorts, Networks and Systems* Dundee: Institute for Research and Innovation in the Social Services. http://www.iriss.org.uk/files/Children1stEvaluation_Final.pdf Accessed August 2009.

Lymbery, M. and Butler, S. (eds) (2004) *Social Work Ideals and Practice Realities*, Basingstoke: Palgrave Macmillan.

Macdonald, G. (1990) 'Allocating blame in social work', *British Journal of Social Work*, 20, 525–46.

(1994) 'Developing empirically-based practice in probation', *British Journal of Social Work*, 24, 405–27.

(2001) *Effective Interventions for Child Abuse and Neglect : An Evidence-Based Approach to Planning and Evaluating Interventions*, Chichester, New York: Wiley.

(2002) 'Evidence-based practice', in Davies, M. (ed.) *Blackwell Companion to Social Work*, Oxford: Blackwell.

(2003) *Using Systematic Reviews to Improve Social Care*, London: SCIE.

Magee, B. (1997) *Confessions of a Philosopher*, London: Weidenfeld and Nicholson.

Mandell, N. (1988) 'The least adult role in studying children' in *Journal of Contemporary Ethnography*, 16 (4).

Mantysaari, M. (2005) 'Realism as a foundation for social work knowledge', *Qualitative Social Work*, 4, 87–98.

Martin, M. (1994) 'Developing a feminist participative research framework' in Humphries, B. and Truman, C. (eds) *Rethinking Social Research:*

Anti-Discriminatory Approaches in Research Methods, Aldershot Avebury.

Maynard, M. (1994) 'Methods, practice and epistemology: the debate about feminism and research' in Maynard, M. and Purvis, J. (eds) *Researching Women's Lives from a Feminist Perspective*, London: Taylor and Francis.

Maynard, M. and Purvis, J. (1994) 'Doing feminist research' in Maynard, M. and Purvis, J. (eds) *Researching Women's Lives from a Feminist Perspective*. London: Taylor and Francis.

McCracken, G. (1988) *The Long Interview Newbury*, Park: Sage.

McIvor, G. (1995) 'Practitioner research in probation' in McGuire, J. (ed.) *What Works? Reducing Offending*, New York: Wiley.

McLaughlin, H. (2007) *Understanding Social Work Research*, London: Sage.

(2009) *Service User Research in Health and Social Care*, London: Sage.

McLeod, J. (1997) *Narrative and Psychotherapy*, London: Sage.

(1999) *Practitioner Research in Counselling*, London: Sage.

McPherson, I., Hunter, D. and McKeganey, N. (1986) 'Interviewing elderly people: some problems and challenges' in *Research, Policy and Planning*, 5 (2).

Mercer, G. (2002) 'Emancipatory disability research' in Barnes, C., Oliver, M. and Barton, L. (eds) *Disabilities Studies Today*, Cambridge: Polity.

Merton, R. (1987) 'The focussed interview and focus groups', *Public Opinion Quarterly*, 51, 550–66.

Midgley, M. (2001) *Science and Poetry*, London: Routledge.

Miller, E. and Gwynne, G. (1972) *A Life Apart*, London: Tavistock Publications.

Mitchell, W. (forthcoming) ' "I know how I feel": listening to young people with life-limiting conditions who have learning and communication impairments', *Qualitative Social Work*.

Moon, G., Gould, M. et al. (2000) *Epidemiology: An Introduction*, Buckingham, Open University Press.

Munro, E. (1998) *Understanding Social Work – An Empirical Approach*, London: Athlone Press.

National Institute of Social Work (1982) *Social Workers. Their Role and Tasks (The Barclay Report)*. Bedford Square Press.

Neander, K. and Stott, C. (2006) 'Important meetings with important persons: narratives from families facing adversity and their key figures' *Qualitative Social Work*, 5 (3): 295–311.

Newman, T., Moseley, A., Tierney, S., and Ellis, A. (2005) *Evidence-Based Social Work: A Guide for the Perplexed*. Lyme Regis: Russell House Publishing.

Noon, M. and Blyton, P. (2002) *The Realities of Work*, Basingstoke: Palgrave.

Norman, R. (1998) *The Moral Philosophers*, Oxford: Oxford University Press.

Oliver, M. (1992) 'Changing the social relations of research production?', *Disability, Handicap and Society*, 7, 101–14.

Panaser, A. (2003) 'Sikhing social work', in Cree, V. (ed.) *Becoming a Social Worker*, London: Routledge.

Parton, N. (1998) 'Risk, advanced liberalism and child welfare: the need to rediscover uncertainty and ambiguity', *British Journal of Social Work*, 28, 5–27.

Parton, N. and O'Byrne, P. (2000) *Constructive Social Work: Towards a New Practice*, Basingstoke: Palgrave Macmillan.

Pawson, R. and Tilley, N. (1997) 'An introduction to scientific realist evaluation' in E. Chelinsky and W. Shadish (eds) *Evaluation for the Twenty-First Century*, Newbury Park CA: Sage.

(1997) *Realistic Evaluation*, London: Sage.

Pawson, R., Boaz, A., Grayson, L., Long, A., and Barnes, C. (2003) *Types and Quality of Knowledge in Social Care*, London: Social Care Institute for Excellence.

Philp, M. (1979) 'Notes on the form of knowledge in social work', *Sociological Review*, 27, 83–111.

Polkinghorne, D. (2004) *Practice and the Human Sciences – The Case for a Judgement-Based Practice of Care*, Albany: State University of New York.

Popper, K. (2002) *Conjectures and Refutations*, London: Routledge.

Preston-Shoot, M. and Wigley, V. (2002) 'Closing the circle: social workers' responses to multi-agency procedures on older age abuse', *British Journal of Social Work*, 32, 299–320.

Prior, L. (2003) *Using Documents in Social Research*, London: Sage.

Radical Statistics (undated) *About Radical Statistics*, Accessed at: http://www.radstats.org.uk/about.htm

Reason, P. (1994) 'Three approaches to participative inquiry' in Denzin, N. and Lincoln, Y. (eds) *Handbook of Qualitative Research*. Thousand Oaks: Sage.

Reid, W. (1988) 'Service effectiveness and the social agency' in Patti, R., Poertner, J. and Rapp, C. (eds) *Managing for Effectiveness in Social Welfare Organizations*, New York: Haworth.

(1998) *Empirically Supported Practice: Perennial Myth or Emerging Reality?* Distinguished Professorship Lecture. New York: State University at Albany.

(2001) 'The role of science in social work: the perennial debate', *Journal of Social Work*, 1, 273–93.

Rhodes, R. A. W. (1997) *Understanding Governance*, Buckingham: Open University Press.

(2008) 'Understanding governance: ten years on', *Organization Studies*, 28, 1243–64.

Riemann, G. (2005) 'Ethnographies of practice – practicing ethnography', *Journal of Social Work Practice*, 19 (1), 87–101.

Riessman, C. and Quinney, L. (2005) 'Narrative in social work: a critical review' in *Qualitative Social Work*, 4 (4), 391–412.

Rodriguez, N. and Ryave, A. (2002) *Systematic Self Observation*, Thousand Oaks: Sage.

Rogers, P. J. and Williams, B. (2006) 'Evaluation for practice improvement and organizational learning' in Shaw, I., Greene, J. and Mark, M. (eds) *Sage Handbook of Evaluation I*, London: Sage.

Rorty, R. (1979) *Philosophy and the Mirror of Nature*, Princeton: Princeton University Press.

Sabatier, P. (1986) 'Top-down and bottom-up approaches to implementation research', *Journal of Public Policy*, 6, 21–49.

Sackett, D., Rosenberg, W., Muir Gray, J., Haynes, R., and Richardson, W. (1996) 'Evidence-based medicine: what it is and what it isn't', *British Medical Journal*, 312, 71–2.

Schon, D. (1983) *The Reflective Practitioner: How Professionals Think In Action*, New York: Basic Books.

Scott, J. (1990) *A Matter of Record: Documentary Sources in Social Research*, Cambridge: Polity.

Scourfield, J. (2001) 'Interviewing interviewers and knowing about knowledge' in Shaw, I. and Gould, N., *Qualitative Research in Social Work*, London: Sage.

Shakespeare, T. (1996) 'Rules of engagement: doing disability research', *Disability and Society*, 11, 1115–19.

(2006) 'The social model of disability' in Davis, L. (ed.) *The Disabilities Studies Reader*, New York: Routledge.

Shaw, I. (1996) *Evaluating in Practice*, Aldershot: Ashgate.

(1999) *Qualitative Evaluation*, London: Sage.

(2004) 'William J. Reid: An appreciation', *Qualitative Social Work*, 3 (2), 109–15.

(2005) 'Practitioner research: evidence or critique?' in *British Journal of Social Work*, 35 (8), 1231–48.

(2008) 'Ways of knowing' in M. Gray and S. A. Webb (eds) *Social Work Theories and Methods*, London: Sage.

(2010) 'Qualitative social work practice research', in Briar-Lawson, K., Fortune, A. and McCallion, P., *Advancing Practice Research in Social Work*, New York: Columbia University Press.

Shaw, I. and Gould, N. (2001) *Qualitative Research in Social Work*, London: Sage.

Shaw, I. and Shaw, A. (1997a) 'Keeping social work honest: evaluating as profession and practice', in *British Journal of Social Work*, 27 (6), 847–69.

(1997b) 'Game plans, buzzes and sheer luck: doing well in social work', in *Social Work Research*, 21 (2), 69–79.

Sheldon, B. (2001) 'The validity of evidence-based practice in social work: a reply to Stephen Webb', *British Journal of Social Work*, 31, 801–9.

Sheldon, B. and Macdonald, G. (1998) 'Changing one's mind: the final frontier?', *Issues in Social Work Education*, 18, 3–25.

(1999) *Research and Practice in Social Care: Mind the Gap*, Exeter: Centre for Evidence-Based Social Services, University of Exeter.

(2008) *A Textbook of Social Work*, London: Routledge.

Sheldon, B., Ellis, A., Mooseley, A. and Tierney, S. (2004) *Evidence-Based Social Care – An Update of Prospects and Problems*, Centre for Evidence-Based Social Care: University of Exeter.

Sheppard, M. (1995) 'Social work, social science and practice wisdom', *British Journal of Social Work*, 25, 265–93.

(1998) 'Practice validity, reflexivity and knowledge for social work', *British Journal of Social Work*, 28, 763–83.

(2004) *Appraising and Using Social Research in the Human Services: An Introduction for Social Work and Health Practitioners*, London: Jessica Kingsley.

(2006) *Social Exclusion and Social Work: The Idea of Practice*, Aldershot: Ashgate.

Sheppard, M. and Ryan, K. (2003) 'Practitioners as rule using analysts', *British Journal of Social Work*, 33, 157–77.

Sheppard, M., Newstead, S., Di Caccavo, A. and Ryan, K. (2001) 'Comparative hypotheses assessment and quasi triangulation as process knowledge assessment strategies in social work practice', *British Journal of Social Work*, 31, 863–85.

Singer, P. (1983) *Hegel*, Oxford: Oxford University Press.

Smith, David (1987) 'The limits of positivism in social work research', *British Journal of Social Work*, 17, 401–16.

(2002) 'The limits of positivism revisited', *Social Work and Social Sciences Review*, 27–37.

(2004) 'Introduction: some versions of evidence-based practice' in Smith, D. (ed.) *Social Work and Evidence-Based Practice*, London: Jessica Kingsley.

Smith, Dorothy (2004a) 'Women's perspective as radical critique of sociology' in Harding, S. (ed.) *The Feminist Standpoint Theory Reader*, New York: Routledge.

(2004b) 'Comment on Hekman's "truth and method": feminist standpoint theory revisited' in Harding, S. (ed.) *The Feminist Standpoint Theory Reader*, New York: Routledge.

Social Services Inspectorate (1991) *Care Management and Assessment: Practitioners' Guide*, London: HMSO.

(2001) *Modern Social Services – A Commitment to Deliver: The 10th Annual Report of the Chief Inspector of Social Services*, London: Department of Health.

Stepney, P. and Popple, K. (2008) *Social Work and the Community – A Critical Context for Practice*, Basingstoke: Palgrave Macmillan.

Stone, E. (1997) 'From the research notes of a foreign devil: disability research in China' in Barnes, C. and Mercer, G. (eds) *Doing Disability Research*, Leeds: The Disability Press.

Strauss, S., Richardson, W., Glasziou, P., and Haynes, R. (2005) *Evidence-Based Medicine*, Edinburgh: Elsevier.

Taylor, C. and White, S. (2000) *Practising Reflexivity in Health and Welfare: Making Knowledge*. Buckingham: Open University Press.

(2001) 'Knowledge, truth and reflexivity: the problem of judgement in social work', *Journal of Social Work*, 1, 37–59.

Tew, J., Gould, N., Abankwa, D., Barnes, H., Beresford, P., Carr, S., Copperman, J., Ramon, S., Rose, D., Sweeney, A., and Woodward, L. (2006) *Values and Methodologies For Social Research in Mental Health*, London: Social Perspectives Network.

Thompson, R. and Holland, J. (2005) ' "Thanks for the memory": memory books as a methodological resource in biographical research' in *Qualitative Research* 5 (2), 201–19.

Thyer, B. (1989) 'First principles of practice research' in *British Journal of Social Work*, 19 (4), 309–23.

Thyer, B. and Wodarski, J. (1998) 'First principles of empirical social work' in Thyer, B. and Wodarski, J. (eds) *Handbook of Empirical Social Work Practice*, New York: John Wiley and Sons.

(2007) *Social Work in Mental Health: An Evidence-Based Approach*, Hoboken NJ: Wiley.

Timmins, N. (1995) *The Five Giants: A Biography of the Welfare State*, London: HarperCollins.

Timms, N. (1983) *Social Work Values: An Enquiry*, London: Routledge.

TOPSS (2002) *The National Occupational Standards for Social Work*, Leeds: TOPSS.

Traylen, H. (1994) 'Confronting hidden agendas: co-operative inquiry with health visitors' in Reason, P. (ed.) *Participation in Human Inquiry*, London: Sage.

Trevithnick, P. (2008) 'Revisiting the knowledge base of social work: a framework for practice', *British Journal of Social Work*, 38, 1212–37.

Trinder, L. (2000) 'Evidence-based practice in social work and probation' in Trinder, L. and Reynolds, S. (eds) *Evidence-Based Practice*, Oxford: Blackwell Science.

Truman, C. (1999) 'User involvement in large-scale research: bridging the gap between service users and service providers?' in Broad, B. (ed.) *The Politics of Social Work Research and Evaluation*, Birmingham, Venture Press.

(2000) 'New social movements and social research' in Truman, C., Mertens, D. and Humphries, B. (eds) *Research and Inequality*, London: UCL Press.

Truman, C., Mertens, D. and Humphries, B. (2000) *Research and Inequality*, London: UCL Press.

Union of the Physically Impaired Against Segregation and the Disability Alliance (1975) *Fundamental Principles of Disability*. Accessed at: http://www.leeds.ac.uk/disability-studies/archiveuk/UPIAS/fundamental%20principles.pdf

Wahlström, J. (2006) 'Narrative transformations and externalizing talk in a reflecting team consultation' in *Qualitative Social Work*, 5 (3), 313–32.

Wasoff, F. and Dobash, R. (1996) *The Simulated Client: A Method for Studying Professionals Working with Client*, Aldershot: Avebury.

Webb, S. (2001) 'Some considerations on the validity of evidence-based practice in social work', *British Journal of Social Work*, 31, 57–79.

White, S. (1997) 'Beyond retroduction? Hermeneutics, reflexivity and social work practice', *British Journal of Social Work*, 27(5), 739–53.

—— (2001) 'Auto-ethnography as reflexive inquiry: the research act as self surveillance' in Shaw, I. and Gould, N., *Qualitative Research in Social Work*, London: Sage.

White, S. and Riemann, G. (in press) 'Researching our own domains: research as practice in "learning organizations"' in I. Shaw, K. Briar-Lawson, J. Orme and R. Ruckdeschel, *Sage Handbook of Social Work Research*, London: Sage.

White, V. and Harris, J. (2007) 'Management', in M. Lymbery and K. Postle (eds) *Social Work: A Companion to Learning*, London: Sage.

Whitmore, E. (1994) 'To tell the truth: working with oppressed groups in participatory approaches to inquiry' in P. Reason (ed.) *Participation in Human Inquiry*. London: Sage.

—— (2001) 'People listened to what we had to say: reflections on an emancipatory qualitative evaluation' in Shaw, I. and Gould, N. *Qualitative Research in Social Work*, London: Sage.

Williams, D. and Gardner, J. (2002) 'The case against "the evidence": a different perspective on evidence-based medicine', *British Journal of Psychiatry*, 180, 8–12.

Wilson, K., Ruch, G., Lymbery, M., and Cooper, A. (2008) *Social Work: An Introduction to Contemporary Practice*, Harlow: Pearson Longman Education.

Witkin, S. (1992) 'Should empirically-based practice be taught in BSW and MSW programs? No!', *Journal of Social Work Education*, 28 (3).

Wootton, B. (1959) *Social Science and Social Pathology*, London: Allen and Unwin.

Zaleswski, M. (2003) 'Feminist epistemology' in Miller, R. and Brewer J. (eds) *The A–Z of Social Research*, London: Sage.

Zeller, R. (1993) 'Focus group research in sensitive topics' in Morgan, D. L. (ed.) *Successful Focus Groups: Advancing the State of the Art*, Thousand Oaks: Sage.

Ziman, J. (1991) *Reliable Knowledge*, Cambridge: Canto.

Index